POCKET

JAKARTA

TOP SIGHTS · LOCAL EXPERIENCES

SIMON RICHMOND, JADE BREMNER

Contents

Plan Your Trip 4

Market in Jakarta (p19)
RIPSA PHOTO/SHUTTERSTOCK ©

Welcome to Jakarta

Jakarta is dynamic, vibrant and chaotic. It's no oil painting, yet charming juxtapositions can be found on every street. Despite the maddening traffic, life here is lived at speed, driven by an industriousness and optimism that's palpable. A microcosm of the nation's 17,000 islands, Jakarta is where Indonesia puts on its best face.

Jakarta nightscape
ALVIAN INDONESIA/SHUTTERSTOCK ©

Top Sights

Merdeka Square

The city's beating heart. **p64**

SAIKO3P/SHUTTERSTOCK ©

Museum Nasional

Indonesia's best museum. **p62**

Ancol Luar Biasa

Superb outdoor recreation complex. **p56**

GILANGTRISTIANO/SHUTTERSTOCK ©

Jakarta War Cemetery

Remembering tragedy with beauty. **p112**

Museum Wayang

Shadowy characters with sticks and string. **p40**

Jakarta's High-End Malls

Great brands in plush surroundings. **p134**

Street Food in Central Jakarta

Dine alfresco with locals. **p66**

Bogor

Colonial retreat that's an ideal day trip. **p136**

Taman Mini Indonesia Indah

Indonesia's myriad cultures in one location. **p108**

Eating

Jakarta is a world-class eating destination. You'll find an amazing choice from oh-so-refined Javanese imperial cuisine to cooked-on-the-spot dishes from street vendors. Other cuisines (especially Asian) are well represented and prices are lower than you'd expect. Many lounges and bars serve creative menus from top chefs.

When to Eat

Indonesians simply eat whenever they are hungry. The idea of it being a family affair or something to share with friends is less common here. However, as the middle class grows, locals are dining out more for pleasure than mere subsistence. This has fuelled a growing number of modestly priced but very good cafes and restaurants.

Typical breakfast and lunch-times in Jakarta are what you'd find in most places – but dinner can be later. Some restaurants stay open until 10pm and beyond, and some lounges and bars offer excellent menus until well after midnight.

Budgets

Expect to pay around 50,000Rp for a main course in a budget restaurant. This rises to between 50,000Rp and 200,000Rp for the majority of casual restaurants, with top-end hotels and restaurants charging more than 200,000Rp for a main course.

Where to Eat

Street stalls offer excellent, fresh local fare, with many vendors operating out of groups of stalls.

As many Jakartans eschew alcohol, there's a large selection of cafes offering coffee drinks. Standards are very high (this is Java!) and most places also serve meals.

Many stylish lounge bars also have ambitious kitchens serving creative dishes late into the night.

Restaurants are as varied in Jakarta as anywhere. From casual eateries with noodle and rice dishes to elaborate venues, there is a huge range of cuisines to choose

ARIYANI TEDJO/SHUTTERSTOCK ©

from. The days when hotels were the only places to go for a fancy meal are long past.

Malls dot the city, especially in the south, and have food courts with international fast food outlets and fancier chains.

Best Indonesian

Warung Ngalam Classic Indonesian dishes done well, served at a single-seater bar. (p101)

Historia Hip, retro restaurant off Fatahillah Sq serving Indonesian mains. (p50)

Warung Daun New Age versions of Indonesian classics served in a lush compound. (p85)

Best International

Por Que No Spanish tapas in a rooftop eyrie. (p88)

OKU High-end Japanese dishes in a minimalist environment. (p88)

Honu Poke Hawaiian-style rice bowls heaped with a choice of salmon, tuna, tofu or chicken. (p121)

Worth a Trip: Afternoon Tea

Lewis & Carroll (☑ 0812 1381 8465; www. lewisandcarrolltea.com; Jl Bumi 4, Kebayoran Baru, Jakarta Selatan; dishes 55,000-125,000Rp; ⊗8am-10pm) has many locally sourced teas. The loose-leaf teas are served in trays of test tubes that you can smell before ordering. The cafe also serves dishes from all-day breakfast classics to organic salads and pastries.

Best Romantic Eats

Shanghai Blue 1920 Lavish furnishings, including exquisite antiques, are the setting for excellent Indonesian-Chinese dining. (p103)

Lara Djonggrang Imperial Indonesian cuisine and seafood, with a beautiful bar. (p86)

Jakarta on a Plate
Gado Gado

Meaning 'mix-mix' in Indonesian the basis of gado-gado is a mixture of vegetables including potatoes, longbeans, spinach and bean sprouts.

The sauce is made from fried and crushed peanuts, sweet palm sugar, garlic, chilies, salt, tamarind and lime juice.

Tofu and tempeh also traditionally form part of the salad, as do hard-boiled eggs.

Toppings include chopped scallions, salad cress, *bawang goreng* (fried shallots) or *krupuk* (deep fried tapioca crackers).

★ Top Three
Gado Gado in Jakarta

Gado Gado Bon Bin (Map p80, G3; ☎021-392 5404; Jl Cikini 4; mains 25,000-35,000Rp; ⏱10am-5pm)

Lenggang Jakarta (Map p70, B5; www.lenggangjakarta.com; Merdeka Sq; mains from 20,000Rp; ⏱10am-11pm)

Plataran Menteng (Map p80, D3; ☎021-2962 7771; www.plataran.com; Jl Cokroaminoto 42; ⏱11am-10pm)

Gado Gado in Jakarta

The cuisine of the Betawi (the original inhabitants of the Jakarta region) is known for its richness.

Gado gado, a dish of steamed bean sprouts and various vegetables, is served with a spicy peanut sauce, is a Betawi original. So is *ketoprak* (noodles, bean sprouts and tofu with soy and peanut sauce), which is named after a musical style, because it resembles the sound of ingredients being chopped.

Ketoprak

Clubs & Bars

If you're expecting the capital of the world's largest Muslim country to be a sober city with little in the way of drinking culture, think again. Bars are spread throughout the city. You'll find rooftop lounge bars, pubs serving excellent meals and clubs partying through the night.

Booze Restrictions

New licences have been implemented for businesses so authorities can monitor and control who is selling alcohol.

Beer sales in convenience shops were banned nationwide in 2015. Although this policy was reversed in Jakarta after protest, many convenience shops in Jakarta have chosen to tread carefully and remain dry.

You'll find beer in some Jakarta supermarkets and minimarts, but it's often almost hidden.

Many restaurants with bars as well as lounges have quietly de-emphasised their alcoholic drinks. 'Mocktails' are prominently featured.

A proposed law that would have prohibited all sales of alcohol in Indonesia was introduced into the legislature by conservative Islamic parties in 2016. In previous years mainstream parties quickly killed such bills, but this time the bill stayed alive until the session ended. Conservatives plan to continue pursuing it.

Clubs

Jakarta was once one of Southeast Asia's biggest clubbing hot spots. This was thanks to a great variety of venues, which hosted internationally renowned DJs on thunderous sound systems. While that still holds true to a certain extent, the scene has been dialled down – you can still go clubbing in Jakarta, just not with the previous raw abandon.

Entrance is typically 50,000Rp to 300,000Rp, which includes one drink

ANDREA PISTOLESI/GETTY IMAGES ©

(many clubs euphemistically call their cover charges the 'first-drink fee'). Clubs open around 9pm, but don't really get going until after midnight; some are only open at weekends.

Some venues have very strict door policies regarding dress code and other intangibles.

Online events listings at www.indoclubbing.com are good for planning; www.jakarta100bars.com provides unvarnished context.

Best Stylish Drinks

Cloud Lounge Sophisticated decadence and flaming cocktails in this hip mainstay of Jakarta's up-market night scene. (p89)

Awan Lounge A romantic garden lounge on top of a roof. (p105)

Potato Head A brilliant warehouse-style bar-bistro. (p128)

Prohibition Nineteen-thirties speakeasy-style bar with a long menu of crafted cocktails. (p127)

Best Bars

Brewerkz Sports bar and microbrewery serving craft brews. (p127)

Eastern Promise Long-running pub that's a pre-club stalwart. (p128)

Lucy in the Sky Cocktails, DJs and a space with pot plants and retro furniture. (p127)

Cloud Lounge Superman-worthy views of the metropolis from the 49th floor of the Plaza tower. (p89)

Best Clubs

Dragonfly Jakarta's poshest club; gets the best touring DJs. (pictured; p126)

Colosseum Club Vast club with a huge dance floor and a 16m-high roof. (p53)

Immigrant Glamorous local and expat crowd and DJs mixing R&B, hip-hop and more. (p89)

Coffee & Tea

Java is so synonymous with coffee that, in many parts of the world, it's the name used for the drink. Certainly coffee is well respected in Jakarta and there are dozens of locally owned and operated places where you can get a superb cup. In Jakarta there's never a need to visit an international chain.

Coffee History

Coffee was introduced to Indonesia by the Dutch, who founded plantations around Jakarta, Sukabumi and Bogor. Because of the country's excellent coffee-growing conditions, plantations began to spring up across Java, as well as in parts of Sulawesi and Sumatra. Early on the prominent coffee was arabica, which took the name of its origin, hence the common names java, mocha (from Yemen) etc. Robusta has replaced arabica as the coffee most grown because it is easier and cheaper to produce – though coffee drinkers say that arabica is far superior.

Third-Wave Coffee

Jakarta has fully embraced the third-wave coffee scene, a movement that celebrates excellent-quality artisanal coffee, and the intricacies of flavours of bean and roast. This appreciation for fine coffee manifests in a number of ways in the city's coffee shops, including brewing methods, and using microroasteries to control the roasting process and flavour of brews and their roast dates.

Some third-wave coffee shops resemble scientists' workshops, proudly displaying a curious range of glass implements and devices for coffee brewing. Coffee aficionados can choose from various manual brewing techniques, from vacuum coffee and Chemex to V60, cafetière/French press and Areopress, plus moka pot, cold brew and more. Beans served should be of the highest quality

DEDE SUDIANA/SHUTTERSTOCK ©

and coffee shops may have a roasting counter with a bar, so that guests can compare flavours with their barista.

All of the above is likely to take place in a minimalist or industrial-chic setting, with owners putting as much thought into the design of the place as the coffee served.

Best Coffee

Bakoel Koffie Coffee in a colonial cafe out of a Graham Greene novel. (p90)

Filosofi Kopi Immortalised by the Indonesian coffee-lover's movie *Filosofi Kopi*; (2015) does a range of hand brews. (p125)

Tanamera Coffee Third-wave roaster using single-origin beans from Indonesia. (p89)

One Fifteenth Coffee Minimalist coffee house with an excellent food menu. (p126)

Best Tea

Kopi Oey Sabang Modelled on a Chinese tea house; enjoy cute little snacks. (p106)

Pantjoran Tea House Many types of teas are available at this this pie-shaped 1928 beauty. (p51)

Coffee Luwak: The Facts

Coffee luwak (*kopi luwak*) is widely marketed to tourists at shockingly high prices. It is supposedly made from coffee beans that are eaten by civets, then excreted and collected. This is meant to produce a milder, richer brew but, in reality, the civets are often kept in appalling conditions. More often, this method isn't used and what's sold is simply robusta that's been over-roasted and then marked up by a factor of 10.

Shopping

Jakarta is a shopper's dream, with around 100 malls and markets selling goods from around the world at all budgets. There are many flashy malls filled with international brands and luxury labels, but Jakarta's real shopping appeal may be in the venues selling excellent arts and crafts from across the nation.

Small Shops

Retail outlets of interest to visitors are scattered about the more up-market neighbourhoods such as Cikini and Menteng. The main exception is Kemang, where you can walk between designer shops and boutiques. Shops grouped by category can also be found, such as a row of plumbing supplies dealers.

Malls

Start with the glossy pair at the Welcome Monument round-about in Menteng. Across the south are huge developments that combine large malls, up-market hotels and condos. They feature major brands, and like malls worldwide are popular places to simply hang out.

Depending on exchange rates, prices can be tempting, although a lot of what you see is sold worldwide. At international chains, prices are fixed. Most have a basement supermarket where you can buy Western goods.

Geared to the masses, these are often older buildings in busy neighbour-hoods where people can browse among dozens of shops and stalls selling textiles, electronics, housewares etc. The air-conditioning can be spotty. Expect to bargain over any price. Items sold with the labels of name brands are often of dubious provenance.

Best Specialist Shopping

Colony Tall mall with a good bookshop and boutique. (p133)

ASIATRAVEL/SHUTTERSTOCK ©

Darmawangsa Square For local designers and smaller boutique-style shops. (p131)

Eiger Adventure Local outdoor brand selling good-quality, inexpensive gear and camping equipment. (p94)

Best Shopping

Grand Indonesia A hugely popular, high-end mall. (pictured; p94)

Plaza Indonesia Luxury brands by the dozen. (p94)

dia.lo.gue artspace A creative boutique with local designer goods. (p130)

Best Arts & Crafts

Sarinah Thamrin Plaza An older department store with an excellent selection of Indonesian handicrafts. (p107)

Pasaraya Huge shop filled with arts and crafts from across the nation. (p133)

Qonita Batik Top-end colourful headscarf creations. (p133)

Best Markets

Petak Sembilan Market Chinatown's exotic back-street market selling everything from birds in cages to smelly durian. (p47)

Pasar Jl Surabaya Woodcarvings, furniture, textiles, jewellery, old vinyl records and many (dubious) antiques. (p94)

Shop Till You Drop

The annual **Jakarta Great Sale** (www.festivaljakartagreatsale.com) is the time to shop until you drop. It runs during June and July, and features bargain prices, midnight events, chances to win goods, and plenty of social and cultural activities.

Top Jakarta Souvenirs

CHARLES O'REAR/GETTY IMAGES ©

Batik

The batik selection is excellent at Sarinah Thamrin Plaza (p107).

Antique Maps

A treasure trove of antique maps awaits at the Bartele Gallery in the Mandarin Oriental Hotel (pictured; p94).

ASIA TRAVEL/SHUTTERSTOCK ©

Jewellery

The Cikini Gold Center is packed with stalls selling all manner of precious goods and jewellery (p94).

Electronics

Mangga Dua Mall is deals on electric gadgets as well as other bargain goods (p54).

Fashion

Boutique ARA showcases fashions by established and up-and-coming local designers (p132).

Architecture

Jakarta's ebb and flow is a lot to digest. There are historical colonial areas and tribal-building designs, open sewers, former Chinese ghettos and modern monoliths – and construction sites where workers create the landscape of the future. Architectural styles are varied and contradictory, but it's all part of Jakarta's allure.

Colonial Architecture

Sadly, no architecture remains from the city before the Dutch invaded – they demolished what was there and replaced it with sturdy stone colonial buildings. Between 1619 and 1949, Jakarta's population was divided into categories according to people's places of origin: Arabs, Chinese, Malay, Sundanese, Balinese and so on. Ethnic-based enclaves were named kampung. While residents may now freely live wherever they wish, some of these areas still exist, including Chinatown, Kampung Melayu and Kampung Bali. Architecturally, the landscape follows its heritage.

Most of Jakarta's impressive colonial architecture is in central Jakarta and further north around Taman Fatahillah. Some of the oldest buildings date back to the Dutch East India Company era.

Modern Architecture

The geometries of Jakarta's urban landscape have changed rapidly since Indonesia became independent in 1945, and the buildings created have helped to reclaim the city's identity.

In more recent years, construction has had a futuristic feel, some of which is labelled 'tropical modernism'. Highlighting the city's wealth disparities, Jakarta has more than 210 gargantuan skyscrapers (especially around the CBD and Jl Jendral Sudirman), with stacked boxes and angular peaks.

ARTIT WONGPRADU/SHUTTERSTOCK ©

Views from these great heights can be thrillingly dramatic, with post-apocalyptic-style scenes during storms. The list of developments goes on, and Jakarta's modern skyline is ever evolving.

Best Modern Buildings

Monumen Nasional The city's most prominent and extravagant landmark. (p50)

Masjid Istiqlal Modernist mosque, which is the largest in Southeast Asia. (pictured; p48)

Gama Tower Jakarta's tallest building with 360-degree views of the city. (p48)

Best Colonial Buildings

VOC Galangan Vestiges of 18th-century Dutch shipyards and warehouses. (p50)

Museum Bahari Information on Jakarta's maritime history housed in 17th-century warehouses. (p48)

Museum Sejarah Jakarta Bell-towered building that was once the heart of the Dutch empire. (p48)

Museum Seni Rupa Dan Keramik Former Palace of Justice building with palm-shaded grounds. (p48).

Jakarta's Skyscrapers

Recent additions to the skyline include the 195m-high Thamrin Nine Tower 1, which looks like mirrored shipping containers have been stacked up into the sky. The 270m-high Menara Astra is another recently opened skyscraper with modest curves and a super-resilient structure in case of earthquakes.

For Kids

Jakarta is not blessed with a wealth of diversions for children. You and your little ones will also have to put up with the heat, crowds and traffic. But as a family travel destination it's not a dead loss either. Check out the expat website Living in Indonesia (www. expat.or.id) for ideas further to those listed here.

Staying Safe

Most Indonesians adore children; however, children may find the constant attention overwhelming so it's best if both kids and adults are prepared for this.

Health standards are low in Indonesia compared to the developed world, but with proper precautions, children can travel safely.

As with adults, contaminated food and water present the most risks – so err on the side of caution when it comes to eating out.

Always be well armed with water, sunscreen and hats: children are more at risk from sunstroke and dehydration.

Planning

Children's seats for cars are rare and, where they exist, sometimes low quality. Take taxis rather than public transport, which can be crowded and confusing.

Nappy-changing facilities usually consist of the nearest discreet, flat surface. Breastfeeding in public is generally acceptable in Jakarta.

Elsewhere take your cue from local mothers.

Hotels and guesthouses often have triple and family rooms, and extra beds can be supplied on demand. Baby beds and highchairs, however, are uncommon. Hotel staff are usually very willing to help and improvise, so always ask if you need something for your children. Larger hotels can arrange child care.

Larger resorts and hotels, such as the DoubleTree by Hilton and the Hotel Indonesia Kempinski, often

GEORGINACAPTURES/SHUTTERSTOCK ©

have special programs and facilities designed to delight and entertain kids, and include lots of activities during the day and evening.

Bring binoculars so young explorers can zoom in on wildlife, rice terraces, temples, world-class surfers and so on. With widespread 4G data and wi-fi, a smartphone or tablet is handy so children can tell those at home about everything they're missing and have an easy escape from the trip itself.

Best Kid-Friendly Attractions

Ancol Luar Biasa A vast theme park with attractions including Seaworld. (pictured; p56)

Merdeka Square Small playgrounds, stands selling treats and even some tame deer. (p64)

Jakarta Planetarium & Observatory Travel to far-flung galaxies. (p82)

Taman Mini Indonesia Indah Explore the entire archipelago at this large park that recreates the nation's myriad cultures in miniature. (p108)

Worth a Trip: Trampolines & High Ropes

Your kids will love letting off steam at the indoor adventure centre **Houbi** (☏021-2765 4571; www.houbii.com; Blok BB, Jl Metro Pondok Indah 3; 2hr from 225,000Rp; ⏰10am-9pm Mon & Wed-Fri, 2-9pm Tue, 8am-9pm Sat & Sun), a football-pitch-sized space of soft adventure. It's filled with trampolines, a foam pit, high-ropes course, climbing wall and a 7m-high slide with a 90-degree drop.

Historical Sites

Jakarta has witnessed practically every dramatic moment leading up to the Indonesia of today. Remnants of that history are still visible in the city's historic buildings, museums and monuments.

HANAFI LATIF/SHUTTERSTOCK ©

Evolution of the City

On 22 June 1527 the great Javanese general Sunan Gunungjati defeated the Portuguese and drove them off from Sunda Kelapa. The location was renamed Jayakarta ('victorious city') and the date is celebrated today as Jakarta's birthday.

In 1610 the Dutch won the right to build a trading warehouse at the port. Over the next 300 years they would build this up into the city of Batavia, the funnel for commerce and wealth for the entire archipelago. In the post-independence era President Sukarno embarked on an ambitious program to remake Jakarta into a world-class capital. Projects included the 'new city' that rises along Jl Thamrin as Jakarta sprawled ever further south.

Best Historical Sights

Taman Fatahillah The city's original public square is ringed by museums. (p46)

Merdeka Square At the centre of the nation's drama for decades. (p64)

Sunda Kelapa Jakarta's historic port still sees a few old sailing ships. (pictured; p129)

Lapangan Banteng This 200-year-old Dutch square is surrounded by imposing government buildings. (p74)

Taman Suropati An elegant residential square surrounded by art-deco mansions. (p82)

Jakarta War Cemetery WWII dead are buried in an island of serenity amid the clamour of South Jakarta. (p112)

Candra Naya Classic 18th-century Chinese building, and the former residence of Batavia's 'Major of the Chinese'. (p46)

Museums & Galleries

Jakarta's solid stock of museums is the place to learn about Indonesia's history and incredibly diverse cultures. The key one is Museum Nasional and there are good institutions devoted to arts and crafts too. If you're in the market to buy a piece of art, then there's a growing number of good commercial galleries.

CREATIVA IMAGES/SHUTTERSTOCK ©

Best for History

Museum Bank Indonesia Has the story of money, but this colonial building also has the story of Indonesia. (p46)

Museum Bahari Displays in beautifully restored 350-year-old warehouses cover the maritime past of Indonesia. (p48)

Museum Sejarah Jakarta Rummage around in the attic of old Batavia in the city's history museum; treasures abound. (p48)

Museum Perumusan Naskah Proklamasi An old colonial mansion has the story of Indonesia's declaration of independence. (p82)

Best Museums

Museum Nasional Indonesia's standout museum tells the story of the nation's diverse cultures. (p62)

Museum Wayang Has an intriguing collection of shadow puppets, once used in storytelling. (p40)

Best Galleries & Crafts

Galeri Nasional Works of art from around the archipelago are displayed along with much-appreciated special shows. (p72)

Museum Macan Indonesia's first modern and contemporary art museum. (pictured; p120)

Museum Layang-Layang A fun family afternoon out with an impressive collection of 600 kites. (p118)

Best Commercial Art Spaces

RUCI Art Space This industrial space in the hip neighbourhood of Senopati hosts a regular rotation of solo and group exhibitions from local artists. (p118)

dia.lo.gue artspace Rough concrete and smooth glass are an ideal backdrop for the contemporary art and design goods on sale here. (p130)

Activities & Tours

Swimming, yoga, massage and walking tours are the main activities in Jakarta. However, Jakarta adventure companies also offer day trips further afield if you're desperate to escape the city smog.

AKHMAD DODY FIRMANSYAH/SHUTTERSTOCK ©

Tours

Jakarta is huge and sprawling so taking a guided tour is a good way to make sense of it. If you do prefer to walk without a guide, follow a walking tour or escape the city for a stroll in the verdant wonderland of Kebun Raya at Bogor (p136).

Before setting off, always make sure you're wearing a hat and have plenty of water, as walking in Jakarta is a sweaty business.

Best Tours

Jakarta Walking Tour (www.jakartawalkingtour. com) Runs six regular walking tours; all come highly recommended and visit markets, food vendors, historical areas and more. The price includes pick-up at your hotel or hostel.

Hidden Jakarta Tours (www.realjakarta.blogspot. com) These eye-opening walking tours around Jakarta's kampungs, the ramshackle communities of the poor, couldn't take you further from Jakarta's sparkling luxury malls. Expect to walk along polluted riverways, into cottage-industry factories and even meet some of the friendly locals, who may offer you tea in their homes.

City Tour Bus (www.trans jakarta.co.id) A good, free way to get a snapshot of the city is to ride around central Jakarta on these double-decker buses (pictured), laid on by the city government. There's no narration, but you can't beat the price or the view.

Best Activities

Livingseas (http://jakarta. livingseas.asia) Go diving around the Thousand Islands off Jakarta's shore.

Gudang-Gudang Yoga Studio Learn an ancient practice in this peaceful sanctuary. (p118)

Best Spas

Jamu Body Treatment An elegant spa that's an escape from the city. (p129)

Bersih Sehat Menteng An everyday spa for a quick refresh. (p101)

Festivals & Events

Jakarta's festivals and events range from those linked to religion, such as Ramadan and Chinese New year, to commercial and arts jollies.

GEORGINACAPTURES/SHUTTERSTOCK ©

Ramadan

During Ramadan Muslims fast during daylight hours. With conservative groups agitating in Jakarta, most businesses lay low and street stalls will stay closed, even if their clientele normally includes many non-Muslims. Exceptions include eateries in hotels, malls and areas like Chinatown. Conversely, after dusk there's a frenzy of eating across the city as people end their fast.

Idul Fitri (Eid), the traditional end of Ramadan, sees large numbers of people leaving Jakarta and travelling to their home villages or going away on holiday.

Chinese New Year

(pictured) Chinese New Year preparations and celebrations are limited to Jakarta's Chinese neighbourhoods, which, in the centre of the city, means Glodok. Expect to see vendors selling lanterns, offerings and seasonal treats. The temples will be busier than usual.

Best Festivals

Java Jazz Festival (March; www.javajazzfestival.com) Held at the Jakarata International Expo in Kemayoran, it attracts acclaimed international artists as well as Indonesian acts.

Jakarta Anniversary (22 Jun) The establishment of the city in 1527 is celebrated with fireworks and the Jakarta Fair at the Jakarta International Expo complex in Kemayoran.

Independence Day (17 Aug) Indonesia's independence is a day of celebration; the parades in Jakarta are the biggest in the country.

Indonesian Dance Festival (early Nov) Features modern and traditional performances at the Taman Ismail Marzuki.

Four Perfect Days

Day 1

Explore Jakarta's early Dutch colonial period starting at **Taman Fatahillah** (p46) and its surrounding museums. Drop by hip cafe **Acaraki** (p53), before heading to **Museum Bahari** (p48) to learn about the city's maritime heritage.

After lunch at **Historia** (p51) check out historical artefacts at **Museum Sejarah Jakarta** (p48) and intricately decorated vintage puppets at **Museum Wayang** (p40). Round off the afternoon at **Museum Bank Indonesia** (p46) to learn about the history of the nation.

Dine on excellent up-market Indonesian fare at **Kunst-kring Paleis** (p85); then leave the past behind as you zoom up into the sky at **Cloud Lounge** (p89).

Day 2

In the relatively cooler temperature of morning, explore the area around **Lapangan Banteng** (p74) to see government buildings dating back to the colonial period and the country's major religious sites. Then enter **Merdeka Square** (p64) and enjoy the sights while taking in the sheer size of the place.

For lunch take your pick from the many vendors at **Restoran Sari Minang** (p75), then visit the **Museum Nasional** (p62), which is packed with treasures gathered from across Indonesia.

Have a pan-Asian feast at **Shanghai Blue 1920** (p103). Round off the day with cocktails at **Awan Lounge** (p105), followed by dancing to oldies at **Jaya Pub** (p106).

Day 3

Duck in and out of temples, alleys and markets in Glodok's **Chinatown**. Refresh at **Pantjoran Tea House** (p51), then lose yourself in the polychromatic textile splendour of **Pasar Glodok** (p54).

Move on to South Jakarta for lunch at **Blue Terrace** (p121). Later browse the boutiques and galleries of the fairly walkable streets of **Kemang**. Take a rest at **One Fifteenth Coffee** (p126), named after the water-to-coffee ratio in the perfect cup.

For dinner choose between the exquisite Indonesian fare at **Nusa** (p124) or the creative pub fare at **Queen's Head** (p122). Later, perhaps after a pit stop to get dressed at your hotel, join the lovelies at uberposh **Dragonfly** (p126).

Day 4

Stroll around **Taman Suropati** (p82), checking out the many posh old mansions as you circle the lake. Look inside one at **Museum Perumusan Naskah Proklamasi** (p82). Then test your bargaining skills at **Pasar Jl Surabaya** (p94), with its bewildering variety of goods new, not so new and possibly old.

Tjikini (p85) is a good spot for lunch, then indulge in some retail therapy at Jakarta's huge high-end malls, such as the **Plaza Indonesia** (p94).

For dinner choose between **Mamma Rosy** (p122) and **FJ on 7** (p123). Round off the evening at the warehouse-style bar-bistro **Potato Head** (p128) or the sophisticated **Leon** (p127) bar.

Need to Know

For detailed information, see Survival Guide p139

Currency
Rupiah (Rp)

Language Spoken
Bahasa Indonesia

Visas
A visa on arrival allows you to stay up to 30 days.

Money
ATMs are common. Exchanging money is easy. Credit cards are accepted at more expensive establishments.

Mobile Phones
Visitors can get SIM cards at the airport, valid for one month, with data (250,000Rp for 5GB, 350,000Rp for 12GB).

Time
Western Indonesian Time (GMT/UTC plus seven hours)

Tipping
Not expected, but a tip of 5000Rp to 10,000Rp (or 10% of the total bill) is highly appreciated.

Daily Budget

Budget: Less than 600,000Rp
Basic room: 400,000Rp
Cheap street meal: 30,000Rp
Transjakarta bus ticket: 10,000Rp

Midrange: 600,000–2,000,000Rp
Room in modern hotel with most amenities: 400,000–1,200,000Rp
Meal at most restaurants: 200,000Rp
Taxi: under 100,000Rp

Top end: More than 2,000,000Rp
Luxury hotel room: 1,200,000Rp
Lavish gourmet night out for two with drinks: 1,500,000Rp
Hire car and driver: 700,000Rp

Useful Websites

What's New Jakarta (www.whatsnewjakarta.com) Details of events and openings.
Lonely Planet (www.lonelyplanet.com/indonesia/jakarta) Destination information, hotel bookings, traveller forum and more.

Advance Planning

Three months before Check current visa requirements; ensure your passport has six months' validity remaining after the date you arrive in Indonesia.

One month before Book accommodation, taking into account where you will be spending most of your time, so you minimise time you spend in traffic.

Arriving in Jakarta

✈ Soekarno-Hatta International Airport (CGK)

From CGK to the city takes 45 minutes to two hours depending on traffic and the final destination. Taxis cost around 220,000Rp to central Jakarta. Alternatively take the train (one way 70,000Rp, 45 minutes, every 20 minutes from 6.20am to 11.20pm) to central Jakarta. Damri buses run to major train stations (40,000Rp).

✈ Halim Perdana Kusama Airport (HLP)

A taxi to central Jakarta costs 100,000Rp. An express train to connect CGK with HLP is expected to be completed by late 2019.

🚍 Train Stations

All the major train stations in Jakarta have metered taxis.

Getting Around

🚍 Bus

The Transjakarta Busway is probably the quickest way of getting around thanks to bus-only lanes, though these can also get clogged with traffic.

🚗 Car & Motorcycle

Car-hire services with drivers are inexpensive. Go-Jek motorbikes are cheap and quicker than other options, but less safe and exposed to the pollution.

🚕 Taxi

A good option for getting around (with air-con!). Blue Bird is the recommended choice. For other firms, make sure your taxi has a meter.

🚲 Bicycle

Only cycle in certain neighbourhoods. Not recommended citywide, as streets are pot-holed and chaotic.

Jakarta Neighbourhoods

Museum Wayang 👁

Kota & Glodok (p39)
In Kota you'll find restored 18th-century architecture and plenty of museums. Vibrant Glodok is the heart of old Chinatown.

Museum Nasional 👁

Jalan Jaksa Area (p97)
Great location for the best of what the city can offer. Gentrification has diversified accommodation and eateries to cater for all budgets.

Jakarta's High-End Malls 👁

South Jakarta (p111)
A vast area with everything from humble villages to posh hotels. Focus on charming suburbs, like Kemang, and the area's nightlife.

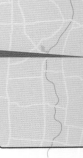

Ancol
Luar
Biasa

**Merdeka Square &
Central Jakarta (p61)**
This huge grassy expanse
is home to Sukarno's
monument to the nation,
and has fine museums and
colonial-era buildings.

Merdeka Square

Street Food in
Central Jakarta

Cikini & Menteng (p77)
Experience Jakarta at
its genteel best. Streets
are tree-lined and canals
seem clean. You'll also
find good cafes, top-end
hotels and malls here.

Jakarta
War
Cemetery

Explore
Jakarta

Street vendor ARDISASTERR/SHUTTERSTOCK ©

Explore

Kota & Glodok

Despite its nooks of fun and culture, to the uninitiated Jakarta can feel overwhelming, but Kota is where the main attractions are easily found. Here live the vestiges of old Batavia, the colonial Dutch city of the 18th century. There are plenty of museums and places to stroll as you survey the city's efforts to reclaim its past even as it plans for the future. Just south, Glodok is the heart of old Chinatown, a busy, compact and vibrant area with temples and markets.

The Short List

○ **Taman Fatahillah (p46)** *Start your exploration of the old town at this colonial square.*

○ **Sunda Kelapa (p49)** *Check out the iconic sailing boats at this centuries-old harbour.*

○ **Museum Wayang (p40)** *Admire the artistry and intricate workmanship of ages-old puppets.*

○ **Jin De Yuan (p46)** *Watch the faithful make offerings at Glodok's premier temple.*

○ **Museum Bank Indonesia (p46)** *See Indonesia's complex past come to life via interactive displays at this museum; history was never this easy or fun.*

Getting There & Around

🚌 Kota is a major stop on several Transjakarta bus lines.

🚗 Depending on traffic, it can take 30 minutes to reach Kota from Menteng and an hour or more from South Jakarta.

🚆 Kota train station has services to points outside of Jakarta.

Neighbourhood Map on p44

Taman Fatahillah (p46) AIYOSHI597/SHUTTERSTOCK ©

Top Sight 📷

Museum Wayang

Before TV, there were puppets. This museum has a vast collection of wayang (flat wooden puppets) from various parts of Indonesia, plus other countries. Its cabinets are full of puppeteering paraphernalia, from the intricate characters used in storytelling to the musical instruments and masks used in performance. The building dates from 1912; previously a Dutch church occupied this spot.

◉ MAP P44, E1

Puppet Museum

☎ 021-692 9560

Taman Fatahillah

adult/child 5000/2000Rp

⏱ 8am-4.30pm Tue-Sun;

👫

Styles of Wayang

There are several styles of *wayang* (pictured), but the two most popular are *wayang kulit* and *wayang golek*. In *wayang kulit* (shadow puppet), elaborate stories are told with the puppets backlit against a screen. In the hands of masters, these performances are dramatic, comedic and can run all night. *Wayang golek* (which unhelpfully translates as 'puppet show') are mostly associated with west Java and involve large and elaborately carved figures that are controlled with various rods.

Hindu Epics

The *wayang* characters are often based on figures from the Hindu epics the Mahabharata and the Ramayana.

In the Mahabharata, the Kauravas are essentially the forces of greed and evil, while the Pandavas – the five acknowledged sons of Pandu – represent refinement and enlightenment. The Pandavas fought and beat the Kauravas in a great war. The svelte figure of Arjuna (a Pandava) is a fitting representative of the noble class, with good looks and a keen sense of virtue. On the Kaurava side, Duryudana, the powerful leader, is too easily influenced by the evil designs of his uncle, Sangkuni. Another character Karna is actually a Pandava, brought up by the rival family – but, adhering to the code of the warrior, he stands by his king and so dies tragically at the hands of Arjuna.

The Ramayana provides well-defined characters such as Rama, the ideal man, and his wife Sita (or sometimes Shinta), the ideal wife. Meanwhile the character of a warrior named Ravana has a brother named Kumbhakarna who is more complex. Kumbhakarna knows that Ravana is evil, but is bound by warrior ethics to support his brother to the grisly end.

A full performance requires hundreds of characters, as you'll see from the displays here.

★ Top Tips

o Various ad hoc performances take place on weekends and can be very worthwhile. Check with the museum for its upcoming schedule.

o Freelance guides can enhance your visit – many of the displays are not well lit, and lack detailed information and context. However, carefully agree on a fee in advance and beware of guides who may try to pressure you into making a puppet purchase at an exorbitant price.

✗ Take a Break

Some of Kota's best food is served up at a range of restaurants around Taman Fatahillah (p46).

Sample a cup of the traditional Indonesian herbal medicinal drink *jamu* at cool cafe Acaraki (p53).

Walking Tour 🥾

Glodok's Chinatown

The neighbourhood of Glodok, the traditional enclave of the Chinese community, is an archetypal city-centre district full of bustling lanes, street markets, a shabby mall or two and oodles of noodle, novelty and herbal remedy vendors. Most of the fun here is simply experiencing the (very) Chinese vibe of the place, eating some dumplings and browsing the myriad stalls.

Walk Facts

Start Museum Bank Mandiri (🚉 Kota)

End Pasar Kemenangan (🚉 Glodok)

Length 1km; one hour

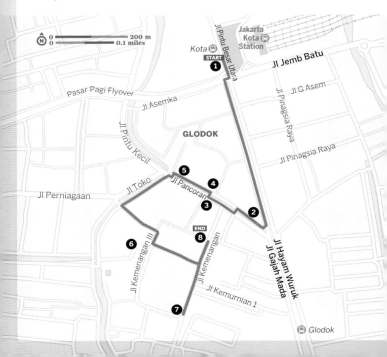

❶ Museum Bank Mandiri

Get into a historic mood at this banking museum (p47). Housed in a fine art-deco structure, it has marble counters, vintage counting machines, abacuses and colossal cast-iron safes. The lack of bells and whistles to the displays adds immeasurably to the period atmosphere.

❷ Pantjoran Tea House

One of the first buildings restored as part of the government program to revitalise the area, this wonderful pie-shaped building makes a good first impression. There are many types of tea on offer at the cafe (p51), as well as a long list of Indonesian and Chinese meals.

❸ Vendors & Shops

Jalan Pancoran is Chinatown's main street. Going west from Jl Gajah Mada, zigzag along both sides of the street to find vendors and small shopfronts where a profusion of goods are sold that defy easy categorisation. It's colourful, smelly, cacophonous and more.

❹ Food Stalls

Plunge into the alleys on the north side of Jl Pancoran, where beautiful displays of familiar produce are interrupted by boiled-intestine vendors and cock's-feet fryers. Wander at random and take your time, as there's plenty to discover.

And, if tempted by a dumpling hawker, bite!

❺ Santong Kuotieh 68

Fried and steamed Chinese pork dumplings are prepared out the front of this very popular little restaurant (p52), which opened in 1968. It may look very basic but they really know what they're doing. The fried pork dumplings are on point: perfectly crispy on the outside and moist on the inside.

❻ Vihara Dharma Jaya Toasebio

This backstreet temple (p50) is heavily scented by the smells of incense and burning offerings.

❼ Jin De Yuan

A large Chinese Buddhist temple (p46) compound that is one of Jakarta's most important. The interior of the main structure is atmospheric with dense incense and candle smoke wafting across Buddhist statues, ancient bells and drums, and some wonderful calligraphy.

❽ Petak Sembilan Market

Take a stroll through Petak Sembilan/Kemenangan Market, situated off Jl Pancoran, and discover stalls piled high with all kinds of fresh produce, including live insects and skinned frogs.

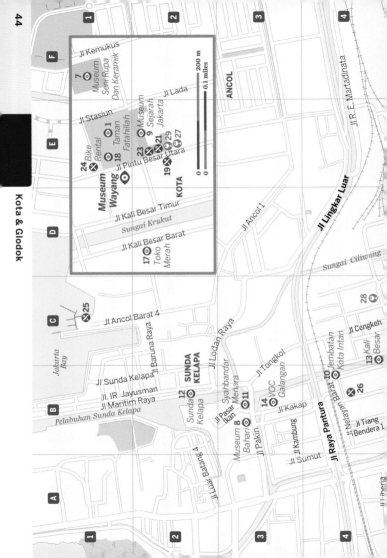

Jl Kemukus

7
Museum
Seni Rupa
Dan Keramik

Jl Stasiun

Jl Lada

24 Bike
Rental

1
Taman
Fatahillah

18

Museum
Sejarah
Jakarta

9

23

Museum Wayang

Jl Pintu Besar Utara

21

29

27

19

KOTA

200 m

0.1 miles

ANCOL

Jl Kali Besar Timur

Sungai Krukut

Jl Kali Besar Barat

17
Toko
Merah

Jl Ancol 1

Jl R. E. Martadinata

Jl Lingkar Luar

Sungai Ciliwung

25

Jl Ancol Barat 4

Jl Baruna Raya

SUNDA
KELAPA

Jl Lodan Raya

Jl Tongkol

28

Jl Cengkeh

Jakarta
Bay

Jl Sunda Kelapa

Jl. IR. Jayusman

Jl Maritim Raya

12
Sunda
Kelapa

Jl Pasar
Ikan

Syahbandar
Menara

11

VOC
Galangan

14

Jl Kakap

Jembatan
Kota Intan

13
Kali
Besar

Pelabuhan Sunda Kelapa

Jl Luar Batang 4

Museum
Bahari

8

Jl Pakin

Jl Kambung

Jl Sumut

Jl Raya Pantura

Nelayan Barat

10

26

Jl Tiang
Bendera 1

Jl Liberia

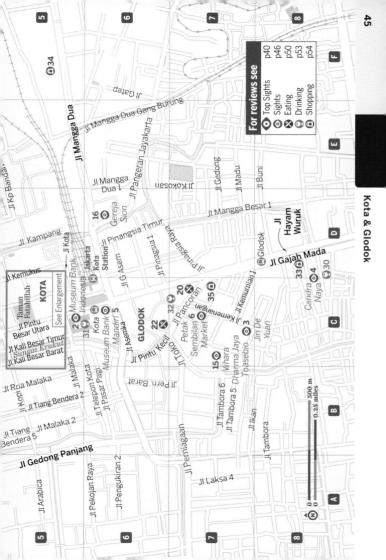

Kota

Taman
Fatahillah

Jl Pintu
Besar Utara

Jl Kali Besar Timur
Jl Kali Besar Barat

Sungai Krukut

See Enlargement

For reviews see

◉	Top Sights	p40
◉	Sights	p46
✖	Eating	p50
🍸	Drinking	p53
🛍	Shopping	p54

Jl Mangga Dua

Jl Mangga Dua Gang Burung

Jl Gatep

Jl Kp Bandan

Jl Kampang

Jl Mangga Dua 1

Jl Pangeran Jayakarta

Jl Kokosan

Jl Mangga Besar 1

Jl Gedong

Jl Madu

Jl Buni

Jl Kota

Museum Bank
Indonesia

Jakarta
Kota
Station

Jl Pinangsia Timur

Gereja
Sion

Jl Pinangsia Timur

Jl Pinangsia Raya

Jl
Hayam
Wuruk

Glodok

Jl Gajah Mada

Jl G Asem

Jl Kemukus

Kota

Museum Bank
Mandiri

Jl Asemka

GLODOK

Jl Pintu Kecil

Jl Tokong

Jl Pancoran

Petak
Sembilan
Market

Jl Kemenangan

Jl Kemunian 1

Candra
Naya

Jin De
Yuan

Jl Pern. Barat

Vihara
Dharma Jaya
Toasebio

Jl Tambora 6

Jl Tambora 5

Jl Ikan

Jl Roa Malaka

Jl Kopi

Jl Malaka

Jl Tiang Bendera 2

Jl Telepon Kota

Jl Pasar Pagi

Jl Tiang
Bendera 5

Jl Malaka 2

Jl Gedong Panjang

Jl Arabica

Jl Pekojan Raya

Jl Pengukiran 2

Jl Perniagaan

Jl Tambora

Jl Laksa 4

0   500 m
0   0.25 miles

Sights

Taman Fatahillah

SQUARE

1 ◉ MAP P44, E1

Kota's central cobblestone square, surrounded by imposing colonial buildings including the former town hall, is where you can get your bearings. You can rent a bike (p50), visit a museum (p40), have a good meal or just wander about amid scores of other visitors, both local and foreign. In Dutch times, this was known as Stadhuis Plein and was the centre of Batavia. Later it was renamed for the commander who captured Sunda Kelapa from the Portuguese in the 16th century. (btwn Jl Stasiun & Jl Pintu Besar Utara)

Museum Bank Indonesia

MUSEUM

2 ◉ MAP P44, C5

This museum presents an engaging and easily consumed history of Indonesia from a loosely financial perspective, in a grand, expertly restored, neoclassical former bank headquarters that dates from the early 20th century. All the displays (including lots of zany audio-visuals) are slickly presented, with exhibits about the spice trade and the financial meltdown of 1997 (and subsequent riots), as well as a gallery dedicated to currency, with notes from every country in the world. (☏021-2600 1588; www.bi.go.id/en/tentang-bi/museum; Pintu Besar Utara 3; 5000Rp; ☺8am-3.30pm Tue-Thu, 8-11.30am & 1-3.30pm Fri, 8am-4pm Sat & Sun)

Jin De Yuan

BUDDHIST TEMPLE

3 ◉ MAP P44, C7

This large Chinese Buddhist temple compound dates from 1755 and is one of the most atmospheric and important in the city. The main structure has an un-usual roof crowned by two dragons eating pearls, while the interior is richly adorned with Buddhist statues, ancient bells and drums, and some wonderful calligraphy. Dense incense and candle smoke wafts through the rooms. (Vihara Dharma Bhakti Temple; Jl Kemenangan; admission free; ☺dawn-dusk)

Candra Naya

HISTORIC BUILDING

4 ◉ MAP P44, C8

Sandwiched in between a Starbucks and modern Novotel hotel is this impressive 18th-century grand residence.

The restored structure has a traditional Chinese curving roof, a tou-kung roof frame and moon gates. Behind it is a tranquil garden with a carp pond. It was the former residence of Khouw Kim An, who was the last 'Mayor of the Chinese' in Batavia.

Inside, visitors can view a few Chinese tapestries and masks, plus portraits of the Khouw family. Look up for the ornate gold detailing on the house's beams. (Jl Gajah Mada 188; free; ☺8am-3pm)

Museum Bank Mandiri
MUSEUM

5 ◉ MAP P44, C6

Having bank museums within a block of each other might have you scratching your head, but it's worthwhile popping in to this one explore the behind-the-scenes inner workings of a bank, and the interior of this fine 1930s art-deco structure. Marvel at the marble counters and vintage counting machines, abacuses, old ATMs and colossal cast-iron safes. Pause on the terrace overlooking the Kota hubbub, before taking the grand staircase up to admire stained-glassed panels and the lavish boardroom.

It's housed in a grand old 10,000-sq-metre building that was once used as the Netherlands Trading Society headquarters. (www.facebook.com/MuseumBank Mandiri; Jl Pintu Besar Utara; adult/child 10,000/2000Rp; ⏱9am-3.30pm Tue-Thu, Sat & Sun, 9-11am & 1-3.30pm Fri)

Petak Sembilan Market
MARKET

6 ◉ MAP P44, C7

Be sure to wander down the narrow Petak Sembilan/Kemenangan Market off Jl Pancoran, lined with crooked houses with red-tiled roofs. It's an assault on the senses, with skinned frogs and live insects for sale next to vast piles of produce. Stalls extend down even narrower neighbouring alleys. (Pasar Kemenangan; Jl Kemenangan; ⏱dawn-dusk)

Jin De Yuan

Museum Seni Rupa Dan Keramik   MUSEUM

7 👁 MAP P44, F1

Built between 1866 and 1870, the former Palace of Justice building is now a fine arts museum. It houses a vast collection of historic Indonesian and Chinese ceramics and Majapahit terracottas, along with contemporary and abstract works by prominent Indonesian artists. Pause and relax in the palm-shaded grounds. (Museum of Fine Arts & Ceramics; 📞021-690 7062; Taman Fatahillah; adult/child 5000/2000Rp; ⏰8am-5pm Tue-Sun)

Museum Bahari   MUSEUM

8 👁 MAP P44, B3

Clost to the entrance to Sunda Kelapa, several old VOC (Vereenigde Oost-Indische Compagnie; the Dutch East India Company) warehouses, dating from 1652, comprise the Museum Bahari. This is a good place to learn about the city's maritime history, with a sprawling series of galleries covering everything from nautical legends and famous explorers to WWII history in the archipelago. Parts of the museum were damaged in a 2018 fire and are being restored; the unaffected areas of the museum remain open.

In the museum you'll find a sextant (used for astronomical navigation), various traditional boats from around Indonesia, the shell of a giant clam, plenty of pickled fish and a lighthouse lamp or two.

The sentry posts outside are part of the old city wall. Also included in the price is entry to the 1839 Syahbandar Menara observation tower, just before the entrance to the maritime museum. (Maritime Museum; 📞021-669 3406; Jl Pakin 1; incl Syahbandar Menara adult/child 5000/2000Rp; ⏰8am-4pm Tue-Sun)

Museum Sejarah Jakarta   MUSEUM

9 👁 MAP P44, E2

Also known as Museum Kesejarahan Jakarta, the Jakarta History Museum is housed in the old town hall of Batavia, a stately whitewashed Dutch colonial structure that was once the epicentre of an empire. This bell-towered building, built in 1627, served the administration of the city and was also used by the city law courts. Inside, it has a collection of artefacts and an impressive 10m painting depicting the attempted siege of Batavia by the Mataram forces in 1628.

In the courtyard at the rear of the building you can head down to its prison cells used during the 19th century to detain various notable Indonesian freedom fighters. (Jakarta History Museum; 📞021-692 9101; Taman Fatahillah; adult/child 5000/2000Rp; ⏰9am-5pm Tue-Sun)

Jembatan Kota Intan   BRIDGE

10 👁 MAP P44, B4

At the northern end of Kali Besar is the last remaining Dutch drawbridge. Built in 1628, it was originally called Hoenderpasarbrug

(Chicken Market Bridge), because it was close to a chicken market. The restored 30m bridge was converted to a drawbridge in 1938 to allow boats to pass and to prevent flooding. You can walk on it for an ideal photo stop. (Kota Intan Bridge; Jl Kali Besar)

Syahbandar Menara
HISTORIC BUILDING

11 ◎ MAP P44, B3

Just before the entrance to the maritime museum is an atmospheric harbourmaster watchtower, built in 1839 to sight and direct traffic to the port. Views include the unappealing landfill and polluted water, but you can still take in some of old Batavia and the chaotic scenes below. Entry includes a visit to the Museum Bahari (Watchtower; off Jl Pakin; incl Museum Bahari adult/child 5000/2000Rp; ⊙9am-3pm Tue-Sun)

Sunda Kelapa
PORT

12 ◎ MAP P44, B2

A kilometre north of Taman Fatahillah (p46), the old port of Sunda Kelapa still hosts magnificent Makassar schooners *(pinisi)*. In some respects the dock scene here has barely changed for centuries, with porters unloading cargo from sailing ships by hand and trolley, though it's far less busy today. There is a more modern main harbour to the right of here, where fancy yachts are docked.

This entire area is rundown and its waters grotesquely polluted. The

Cool Off, Take It Easy

Take your time. It's hot, the streets and traffic are hectic, and things can be intimidating. Plus, large parts of Kota and Glodok are depressingly polluted, but you can fully appreciate all that's here if you keep stress at bay. There's always a place to pause, have refreshments and cool off while you collect your thoughts and digest everything around you.

many tracts of landfill suggest that redevelopment may not be far off.

A local guide named Yuda runs informative tours (☎0812 8108 8277; 3hr tour per person 700,000Rp) around the area. (Jl Maritim Raya)

Kali Besar
CANAL

13 ◎ MAP P44, C4

The Kali Besar is an 18th-century canal built along the Ciliwung River, connecting the port to the old city of Batavia. It once thrived with commerce, and boats shuttled goods to and from the port. Almost 300 years ago it was lined with houses of Batavia's rich and famous. Today you can still see traces of this era in buildings in various stages of restoration and decay along the canal.

The water is filthy, but squint a little and you can sense how the area could look after some investment and a clean-up. (Jl Kali Besar Barat)

VOC Galangan
HISTORIC SITE

14 MAP P44, B3

You can still see vestiges of the 18th-century Dutch shipyards and warehouses that stood on this site. The main building dates from 1628 and has been restored. You can freely wander about and ponder the thick brick walls. The rear area that's a good shaded, grassy area that's a good place for a break. (Jl Kakap I 1-3; free; ⏰10am-5pm)

Vihara Dharma Jaya Toasebio
BUDDHIST TEMPLE

15 MAP P44, C7

Shielded by a narrow opening, this backstreet temple feels like a secret discovery. It is heavily scented with the smells of incense and burning offerings. Respectful visitors are welcome to take a look inside. (Jl Kemenangan III 48; free; ⏰dawn-dusk)

Gereja Sion
CHURCH

16 MAP P44, D6

Dating from 1695, this is the oldest remaining church in Jakarta. Also known as Gereja Portugis (Portuguese Church), it was built just outside the old city walls for slaves captured from Portuguese trading ports. The exterior of the church is very plain, but inside there are copper chandeliers, a baroque pulpit and the original organ. It still holds services every Sunday. (Jl Pangeran Jayakarta; free)

Toko Merah
HISTORIC BUILDING

17 MAP P44, D2

One of the more impressive buildings in Kota is the red-tiled facade of Toko Merah (or 'Red Shop'), which dates back to 1730. It was once the home of Governor-General van Imhoff, when he was in charge of the Dutch East Indies. It got its colour in 1851. It's worth a closer look if you are in the area. (Jl Kali Besar Barat)

Bike Rental
CYCLING

18 MAP P44, E1

Ride around Kota on a brightly coloured, big-tyred Dutch-style bike. You can't miss the stands set up on various edges of the square. The rental fee includes the use of a broad-brimmed straw hat. Let the selfies commence! (Taman Fatahillah; per 30min 20,000Rp; ⏰9am-sunset)

Eating

Historia
INDONESIAN $

19 MAP P44, E2

Served in hip, tiled warehouse environs with soaring ceilings, big art murals and a retro-industrial vibe, Historia's dishes hail from around the archipelago. Try *bandeng goreng sambal* (grilled milkfish with steamed rice and Balinese sambal), *sate ayam* (grilled chicken satay with rice and peanut sauce), *bakmie godog Jawa* (javanese noodles with a spicy broth) and plenty of tasty mixed-rice dishes. (☎021-690 4188; Jl Pintu Besar Utara 11; mains 40,000-51,000Rp; ⊗10am-9pm Mon-Fri, to 10pm Sat & Sun; 🛜)

Pantjoran Tea House   CAFE $

20 ☒ MAP P44, C7

One of the first buildings restored as part of the government program to revitalise the Old Town, this pie-shaped 1928 beauty makes a good first impression for Glodok visitors. Aside from the many types of tea on offer, there's a long list of Indonesian and Chinese meals (from nasi goreng and dumplings to carp with sweet-and-sour sauce). (☎021-690 5904; Jl Pintu Besar Selatan 1; mains 30,000-90,000Rp; ⊗9am-9pm)

Kedai Seni Djakarté   INDONESIAN $

21 ☒ MAP P44, E2

One of several similar places around Taman Fatahillah (p46), this restaurant is housed in a cute old Dutch building with green shutters. You can eat inside under the ceiling fans or people-watch at the outdoor tables. The cheap and tasty dishes are classic Indonesian comfort food, plus there are fresh juices and sweet treats like profiteroles and Indonesian fritters.

Mains include rice dishes like *nasi goreng daging* (smoked beef rice) and *nasi pecel* (steamed rice, bean sprouts, long beans, cabbage, carrot, peanut sauce and soybean cake). (☎0818 0837 4431; Jl Pintu Besar Utara 17; mains 27,000-49,000Rp; ⊗9am-9pm Sun-Thu, to 10pm Fri & Sat)

Toko Merah

Dining Options

You'll find good options for refreshments and meals dotted around Kota and Glodok. Street stalls provide the most convenient fare in Glodok where the alleys off Jl Pancoran (Map p44, C7) are crowded with vendors selling Chinese snacks and meals that are both familiar and intriguingly obscure. In the Taman Fatahillah (p46) area, there are several atmospheric restaurants serving local and international meals.

Santong Kuotieh 68   CHINESE $

22 MAP P44, C6

You'll see cooks preparing fried and steamed Chinese pork dumplings out the front of this ramshackle but highly popular little place, dating back to 1968. Don't be put off by appearances – it's very basic but they really know what they're doing here. The fried pork dumplings are on point: perfectly crispy on the outside and moist on the inside.

Dip them in the house-made sauce – made using 10 spices. The *bakso ikan isi* (fish balls) are also good and there's a range of noodle, rice and vegetable dishes and more to choose from. (0812 3452 9019; www.santong68.com; Jl Pancoran Raya III 4; mains from 35,000Rp, 10 dumplings 45,000Rp; 10.30am-8.30pm)

Bangi Kopi   INDONESIAN $

23 MAP P44, E2

Along the historical pedestrianised strip off Taman Fatahillah (p46), Bangi Kopi is a slick affair with a lot of money poured into its renovation. It's a mishmash of styles that are a bit on the gaudy side, yet prices are reasonable and it does decent Indonesian, Malay and Chinese dishes – from dim sum and rice dishes to noodles. (Jl Pintu Besar Utara 14; mains 25,000-50,000Rp; 8am-11pm;)

Café Batavia   INTERNATIONAL $$

24 MAP P44, E1

This 200-year-old building overlooking Kota's old Dutch quarter pulls crowds. It looks the part, with its classy bistro styled with colonial decor, old parlour floors, marble tabletops and art-deco furnishings. The jazz soundtrack adds to the atmosphere. There may be better places to eat around the square, but for ambience you've hit the jackpot.

The large menu offers Asian and Western dishes, with a choice of small, medium and large sizes for the mains. Service can be slow. There's live music in the evenings, and in the afternoon on Saturdays. (021-691 5531; www.cafebatavia.com; Jl Pintu Besar Utara 14; mains 65,000-185,000Rp; 9am-midnight Sun-Thu, to 1am Fri & Sat;)

Marco Polo Dining Room

INTERNATIONAL $$

25 MAP P44, C1

To the right of Sunda Kelapa (p49) and overlooking the new Batavia Marina, where you'll see a number of modern yachts docked, this dining room has a nautical colonial elegance and serves burgers, pizzas, seafood and Asian dishes. Ask for a table with a view of the Java Sea. (021-691 5599; www.bataviamarina.com/home/marcopolo-room; Batavia Marina, Jl Baruna Raya 9; dishes 60,000-200,000Rp; 10am-10pm)

Restoran Cahaya Mentari

CHINESE $$

26 MAP P44, B4

A classic Chinese restaurant with large tables suitable for banquets, seating 10 people. The atmosphere is pretty dismal, with dated decor and fluorescent lighting. However, the menu has a huge range of classic Chinese dishes and the chefs are very talented. It's in a quieter area just west of Kota. (021-692 2339; Jl Roa Malaka Utara 49; mains 45,000-160,000Rp; 9am-10pm)

Drinking

Acaraki

COFFEE

27 MAP P44, E2

Hidden in a renovated building near Taman Fatahillah (p46), Acaraki is the coolest cafe in the area. It's has exposed brickwork and an enormous wicker lampshade, and serves coffee plus the traditional Indonesian medicinal drink *jamu* (a herbal infusions of roots, bark, flowers, seeds, leaves and fruits) believed to have health benefits. (www.acaraki.com; Gedung Kerta Niaga 3, Kota Tua, Jl Pintu Besar Utara 11; jamu from 18,000Rp; 10am-10pm)

Colosseum Club

CLUB

28 MAP P44, C4

Next to 1001 Hotel, this vast club with a huge dance floor and a 16m-high roof is the venue for one of the most impressive lighting systems in the world. Trance, house, retro and foam are just some of the elements of the spectacle. Somewhat up-market, there's still a hint of sleaze around the edges. (021-690 9999; http://colosseum.id; Jl Kunir 7; from 80,000Rp, event prices vary; 10pm-5am Wed-Sat)

Warung Umak

COFFEE

29 MAP P44, E2

Walk under an arched doorway to find this inconspicuous little place with minimal chic decor, chunky wooden tables, exposed concrete walls, coloured metal chairs and long hanging lights. It serves a range of espresso drinks and manual brew coffees, plus Indonesian mains and blended ice drinks. (Jl Pintu Besar Utara 6-8, Kota Tua; drinks/mains from 12,000Rp/17,000Rp; 10am-9pm Tue-Sun, to 8pm Mon)

Kopi Oey Candra Naya CAFE

30 MAP P44, D8

A branch of the hip 1920s-themed local coffee shop sits on a quiet lane to the south of Candra Naya (p46). It serves a decent cup of coffee, plus Indonesian and Western mains like rice dishes, and breakfasts such as French toast drenched in syrup. (021-2937 9290; http://kopitiamoey.com; Green Central City, Jl Gajah Mada 188; menu items & coffee from 20,000Rp; 9am-midnight)

Canteen CAFE

31 MAP P44, C6

If looking around the Museum Bank Indonesia (p46) and Museum Bank Mandiri (p47) leaves you in need of a pick-me-up, this little cafe sandwiched between both sights will do the job. It has mismatched furniture and serves inexpensive local eats (rice and noodle dishes), coffee, fresh juices and smoothies. (Jl Pintu Besar Utara; coffee/dishes from 17,000Rp/22,000Rp; 9am-6pm Tue-Sun;)

Kopi Es Tak Kie COFFEE

32 MAP P44, C7

Offering coffee where you least expect it, this Glodok stalwart in the heart of the Petak Sembilan Market (p47) opened in 1927. Patrons sit on mismatched plastic stools under unforgiving fluorescent lights, but one sip of the house-roasted custom blend and you'll forget everything around you. It sells simple Indonesian noodles and rice dishes too. Weave through the alleys to get here. (021-692 8296; www.kopiestakkie.com; Jl Pintu Besar Selatan III, Gang Gloria 4-6; menu items & coffee from 20,000Rp; 6.30am-2pm)

Shopping

Maxim Fruit Market FOOD & DRINKS

33 MAP P44, D8

This particularly good grocery sells all manner of Southeast Asian fruits from dragonfruit and mangosteen to durian, guava and rambutan. It also stocks Western imports like granola and Nutella, and more unusual produce like packets of salted egg-fish skin. Its range of single-origin chocolate from Indonesia is excellent. (021-633 7737; Jl Gajah Mada 189-190; Indonesian chocolate from 20,000Rp; 8am-11pm)

Mangga Dua Mall MALL

34 MAP P44, F5

The place for electronics (and exotica such as Russian watches), Mangga Dua Mall is a busy combination of six adjoining multistorey malls. You'll also find cheap textiles and even cheaper foodstuffs. (Jl Mangga Dua; 9am-6pm)

Pasar Glodok MALL

35 MAP P44, C7

A hectic old-school mall with spotty air-con but enough textiles to blanket the city. Plunge into the narrow aisles between the polychromatic stalls. (Jl Gajah Mada; 7am-7pm)

From Pakuwan to Jakarta: Birth of a City

Though evidence exists of human habitation in Jakarta from prehistoric times, it was not until the 12th century that a settlement at the mouth of the Ciliwung River rose to prominence. The Hindu-Buddhist Pajajaran kingdom, whose capital of Pakuwan was upriver near present-day Bogar, established the port of Sunda Kelapa as a trading centre. Like many ports in the archipelago, through trade it came in contact with influences from India, China and Arabia, and the religions of Hinduism and Buddhism and, later, Islam.

Drawn by the port, the Portuguese arrived in 1522 and started a colony, only to be driven off a few years later by Sunan Gunung-jati, the Muslim saint and leader of Demak. He renamed the city Jayakarta, meaning 'victorious city', and it became a fiefdom of the Banten sultanate.

At the beginning of the 17th century the Dutch and English jostled for power in the city, and in late 1618 the Jayakartans, backed by the British, besieged the VOC (Vereenigde Oost-Indische Compagnie) fortress. The Dutch managed to fend off the attackers until May 1619 when, under the command of Jan Pieterszoon Coen, reinforcements stormed the town and reduced it to ashes. A stronger shoreline fortress was built and the town was renamed 'Batavia' after a tribe that once occupied parts of the Netherlands in Roman times. It soon became the capital of the Dutch East Indies.

Within the walls of Batavia the prosperous Dutch built tall houses and pestilential canals in an attempt to create an Amsterdam in the tropics. By the early 18th century, the city's population had swelled, boosted by both Javanese and Chinese eager to take advantage of Batavia's commercial prospects.

By 1740 ethnic unrest in the Chinese quarters had grown to dangerous levels, and on 9 October violence broke out on Batavia's streets; around 5000 Chinese were massacred. A year later Chinese inhabitants were moved to Glodok, outside the city walls. Other Batavians, discouraged by severe epidemics between 1735 and 1780, also moved, and the city began to spread far south of the port.

Top Sight 📷
Ancol Luar Biasa

On Jakarta's bayfront, the people's 'Dreamland' is a vast recreation complex. The largest of its kind in Southeast Asia, it has amusement rides, theme parks and sporting and leisure facilities. Families can easily lose themselves for a day of (primarily) watery fun.

Dreamland
📞 021-2922 2222
www.ancol.com
Jl Pantai Indah
basic admission 25,000Rp
🕐 24hr; 🚻

Dunia Fantasi

This fun theme park (Fantasy Land; Mon-Fri 200,000Rp, Sat & Sun 295,000Rp; ⊙10am-6pm Mon-Fri, 9am-8pm Sat & Sun; 👪) has a very Disneyland-esqe 'main street' entrance, and the Puppet Castle is a straight 'It's a Small World' replica. But the Indonesian influence prevails – Western World is the old west complete with a 'rumah jahil' (jailhouse) for miscreants. The 30 rides include the spectacular Halilintar twisted roller coaster, the Niagara flume, a *Star Wars* adventure and a Ferris wheel. A robot theatre tells stories about Indonesia.

Seaworld Ancol

This vast aquatic park (pictured; Jl Lodan Timur 7; Mon-Fri 140,000Rp, Sat & Sun 160,000Rp; ⊙9am-6pm; 👪) includes a 'Sharkquarium', lethargic but captivating dugongs and turtles. Unaffiliated with the US version of Seaworld, this one is best known for the 'Antasena tunnel', a huge plexiglass tube that enables you to walk through the middle of an enormous aquarium.

Atlantis Water Adventure

Yes, like everything else here, it's big! This waterpark (Mon-Fri 120,000Rp, Sat & Sun 175,000Rp; ⊙8am-6pm Mon-Fri, 7am-6pm Sat & Sun; 👪) complex has eight separate areas, including a wave pool, waterslides and a slide pool, plus artificial beaches (which are a lot cleaner than the nearby 'natural' beaches).

Pasar Seni

Meet craftspeople and find arts and crafts from all over Indonesia at this market that also has cafes and a gallery where there are often interesting exhibitions.

★ Top Tips

○ The Gondola, a cable-car system, provides great views of the bay and the entire complex.

○ Do everything possible to avoid visiting on weekends.

○ Pasar Seni is included in the basic admission; every other major attraction charges separately.

✕ Take a Break

There's an international restaurant and bar at the park's **Mercure Convention Center Ancol** (☏021-640 6000).

★ Getting There

🚌 Three Transjakarta bus lines (5, 5A, 7B) run to Ancol.

🚕 It will cost around 70,000Rp from Jl Thamrin.

Walking Tour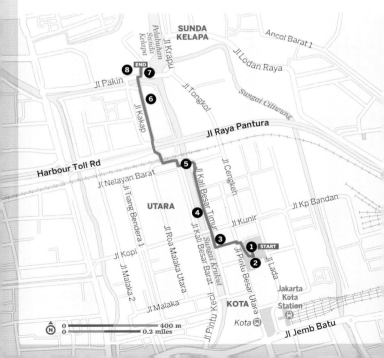

Strolling Old Batavia

On this walk around the old waterways of Sunda Kelapa you'll see the vestiges of the earliest incarnation of Jakarta. The centre of power for the Dutch East Indies during the 17th and 18th centuries was Batavia's port. Disease from the area's polluted canals and swamps forced the Dutch to shift the city centre to today's Merdeka Square in the early 1800s. What they left behind has been crumbling away since.

Walk Facts

Start Taman Fatahillah (Kota)

End Museum Bahari

Length 1km; two hours

❶ Taman Fatahillah

In Dutch times, this cobblestone square (p46), surrounded by imposing colonial buildings, was known as Stadhuis Plein and was the centre of Batavia. Later, it was renamed for the commander who captured Sunda Kelapa (p49) from the Portuguese in the 16th century.

❷ Museum Sejarah Jakarta

On the south side of the square, Jakarta's history museum (p48) is housed in Batatvia's old town hall. This stately Dutch colonial structure with a bell tower was the epicentre of an empire when it was built in 1627. Inside, you'll feel like you're rummaging through old Batavia's attic as you survey the dusty collection of artefacts.

❸ Dharma Niaga Building

Cross the square to the north-west and walk along the south side of the landmark Dharma Niaga Building. Built in 1912, it housed an insurance company and has been restored as part of a city-funded effort.

❹ Kali Besar

Turn north and walk along the side of this 18th-century canal (p49), built along the river, on which boats carried goods to and from the port. Today you can still see vestiges of colonial Dutch buildings along the canal (which is still polluted).

❺ Jembatan Kota Intan

At the northern end of Kali Besar, take a photograph of the last Dutch drawbridge (p48). Originally called Hoenderpasarbrug (Chicken Market Bridge), it dates from the 17th century.

❻ VOC Galangan

Along Jl Kakap look out for what remains of the 18th-century Dutch shipyards and warehouses. The restored main building (p50), which dates from 1628, has a shaded grass area to the rear.

❼ Syahbandar Menara

Continue north across very busy Jl Pakin towards the atmospheric harbourmaster watchtower (p49), built in 1839. Climb up for area views.

❽ Museum Bahari

End your stroll at the maritime museum (p48). The wonderful 17th-century buildings (some renovated) are often echoingly empty. The best exhibits are near the entrance, where models show what old Batavia looked like. Things have changed!

Explore ◈
Merdeka Square & Central Jakarta

Welcome to the proud political centre of the nation. Think of Merdeka Square as sprawling Jakarta's bullseye, and the national monument (Monas) as the dart. Monas was Indonesia's first president Sukarno's gift to the nation. The square is a huge grassy expanse and is surrounded by good museums and some fine colonial-era buildings.

The Short List

○ **Merdeka Square (p64)** *Encounter decorative pools, trees, soaring Monas and more at the heart of Jakarta.*

○ **Museum Nasional (p62)** *Visit Indonesia's best museum, which brings together treasures from across the nation's 17,000 islands.*

○ **Galeri Nasional (p72)** *See works by some of the best Indonesian artists, especially during special exhibits.*

○ **Lenggang Jakarta (p74)** *Sample superb street foods at these well-managed open-air food courts.*

○ **Lapangan Banteng (p74)** *Witness the old Dutch splendour of the government buildings surrounding this square.*

Getting There & Around

🚌 Several Transjakarta lines run along the west side of Merdeka Square.

🚈 Jakarta's busiest train station, Gambir, is on the east side of Merdeka Square.

Neighbourhood Map on p70

Monumen Nasional (p65) SAIKO3P/SHUTTERSTOCK ©

Top Sight 📷
Museum Nasional

The National Museum is the best of its kind in Indonesia and an essential visit. It brings together treasures from the incredible diversity of cultures across the nation's 17,000 islands. The collection sprawls across a series of rooms and buildings; explanatory information is variable.

◉ MAP P70, B4

National Museum

📞 021-386 8172

www.museumnasional.or.id

Jl Medan Merdeka Barat 12

10,000Rp

🕗 8am-4pm Tue-Fri, to 5pm Sat & Sun

Archaeology Courtyard

The enormous collection begins around an open courtyard of the 1862 building, which is stacked with magnificent millennia-old statuary including a colossal 4.5m stone image of a Bhairawa king from Rambahan in Sumatra, who is shown trampling on human skulls. The stunning display of stone sculptures continues around the grassy verge. Ironically, many are here because the Dutch spirited them away but then returned them, which meant they were spared from scavengers.

Architecture Room

Behind the Inner Courtyard, pass through an often-crowded open-air seating area and duck through large wooden doors to the Architecture Room, which is part of the very large ethnography collection. Here you'll find dozens of models showing the incredible range of structures and building styles found across the archipelago. The lighting could be better, but here are the spectacular creations of Tana Toraja in Sulawesi, Pulau Nias off Sumatra, and the Batak and Minangkabau areas of Sumatra. It will likely make you want to book onward travel tickets.

Textile Collection

In a side room off the inner courtyard, the textile collection (koleksi tekstil) has beautiful fabrics including koffo from Sulawesi, an intricate woven cloth with rich gold threads.

Candi Brahu Collection

Over in a spacious modern wing, there are four floors with sections devoted to the origin of humankind in Indonesia. Don't miss the superb display of 9th-century gold treasures from Candi Brahu in Central Java: glittering necklaces, elaborate armbands (note the climbing vine motif signifying the fertility of Java) and a bowl depicting scenes from the Ramayana.

★ **Top Tips**

o The Indonesian Heritage Society (www.heritagejkt.org) organises free English tours of the National Museum at 10am on Tuesdays, Wednesdays, Thursdays and Saturdays, with an additional tour on Thursdays at 1.30pm. Consult the website for the latest schedule.

o Try to avoid visiting on Sundays when huge numbers of families pour in.

o The museum's nicknamed the 'Ganesh Museum' for the large bronze elephant out the front.

✗ **Take a Break**

There's a small cafe in the modern wing of the museum serving basic snacks and hot drinks.

Just a 10-minute walk away, in the southwest corner of Merdeka Square, there's 50-plus cheap-and-cheerful food stalls where you can sample dishes from across the archipelago.

Top Sight 📷
Merdeka Square

Merdeka Square (Independence Square) has become known as the figurative centre of Jakarta. The 1-sq-km green space is one of the largest squares in the world, with big lawns on which to unwind from hectic city life. Named Koningsplein (Kings Square) when the Dutch ruled, officials took up residence in the grand buildings surrounding the square when Batavia collapsed.

◎ **MAP P70, C4**

Lapangan Merdeka

Jl Merdeka Selatan

Monumen Nasional

In the centre of Merdeka Square stands the distinctive 132m-high **National Monument** (Map p70, C4; adult/student/child 15,000/8000/4000Rp; ☉ lift 8am-4pm & 7-10pm). Also known as Monas, it's the city's most prominent and extravagant landmark, and the final gift from former president Sukarno. Construction began in 1961, but Monas was not completed until 1975, when it was officially opened by Sukarno. The monument is made from Italian marble and topped with a sculpted flame, gilded with 50kg of gold leaf. Entrance to the monument is via an underground tunnel below the huge terrace; follow the crowds.

It's best to avoid weekends, when you might be standing in queues for as long as several hours. The lift to the top of the monument leaves every hour (with the exception of 5pm and 6pm). There's capacity for 600 at the top. If you'd rather not queue, you can just walk up to the goblet – the first platform on the monument – for a lower view over the square.

A section in the base is devoted to a small history museum with dioramas of notable moments in Indonesian history.

Gardens

Once home to many government buildings, a concerted effort was made to clear the area and create lawns and gardens by the mid-1990s. Merdeka was used for protest rallies during the upheavals of 1998, and in 2002. The government took a dim view of using the square for protests, so the authorities decided to build a massive iron fence around the square, which you can still see today; access (and egress) is often hampered by this barrier. Still, when you stroll under the trees, watch kids play pick-up football, and delight in a simple meal, you'll fully appreciate this grand expanse.

★ Top Tips

○ Various main entrance gates to the square may be closed, depending on official events, protests and so on taking place in the area. Check with the park guards about which ones will be open before you start walking across the enormous expanse.

○ Don't expect to find many eating options outside of Merdeka's food court area; carry your own water.

○ Dozens of small spotted deer wander a large tree-shaded enclosure in the southeast corner of the park.

✕ Take a Break

If you'd like a meal in air-con comfort, try Padang-style eatery Restoran Sari Minang (p75), about a 10-minute walk northeast.

Search out Lulu & Kayla Cakes (p75) for a ridiculously good cupcake.

Top Sight 📷
Street Food in Central Jakarta

If Indonesian democracy seems to progress in fits and starts, there's one place where it can be said that the people truly rule: at a street-food vendor. Patronised by Indonesians from all walks of life, unprepossessing street food stalls are the place to gleefully feast on seemingly humble dishes whose provenance and relative quality is debated with a heat matched only by the flames beneath the sizzling wok.

🏃 If you're staying in central Jakarta, street-food stalls, such as Lenggang Jakarta (p74) are within walking distance.

🚕 From outside central Jakarta, you can access them by taxi.

Night Markets

By day you see a few panels leaning against walls and maybe the odd broken plastic chair. But come night and suddenly that ignored patch of pavement teems with activity as hundreds of cooks and diners jostle amid dozens of stalls and a cacophony of food-frying and soup-slurping. Long after midnight you can enjoy fantastic freshly cooked fare. The Jl KH Wahid Hasyim Food Stalls (p101) is a small but central night market worth trying.

Food Alleys

Even in the smartest parts of town you can follow your nose to alleys filled with vendors serving the masses. Jalan Kampung Lima Food Stalls (p101) shelter in the shadow of the capital's biggest bank buildings. Feast amid the colonial-era buildings of Kota at the Taman Fatahillah Food Stalls (p46). Merdeka Square (p64) is also the location of the foodie heaven Lenggang Jakarta (p74).

What to Eat

Indonesia's national dish nasi goreng (fried rice) is prepared in almost as many ways as there are street stalls that sell it (meaning: zillions). *Roti bakar* (grilled bread) may sound humdrum until Jakarta's street chefs and street eaters get hold of it. Try it savoury, filled with cheese, sausage or eggs, or sweet with a smear of fruit or coconut jam. There are also thousands of varieties of sweet and savoury *jajanan* (snacks) sold everywhere and made from almost anything and everything: peanuts, coconuts, bananas, sweet potato etc. They are cheap, so sample at will.

★ Top Tips

o Follow the crowds: Jakarta's savviest diners vote with their rupiah. At huge street-food bazaars such as the unmissable Lenggang Jakarta, some of the dozens of stalls are far more equal than others.

o Stuck in traffic? (Need we ask?) Do like any good Jakartan and pull over at the first street-food vendor you see to order some refreshments and a snack. The vendor will happily hand you the goods through your window.

o Is street food safe? Listen to your own intuition. If you think the vendor seems sketchy, skip on by. Order fresh. A treat right out of boiling oil is less likely to be tainted than something that's been sitting around waiting to be bought.

Walking Tour

Exploring the Heart of Indonesia

Here in the very heart of Jakarta is the evidence of the progressive vision of Indonesia's first president, Sukarno. Dutch colonial buildings from the 19th century were repurposed for the new republic while he ordered grand construction schemes to change the city's fabric. On this walk you'll see the official heart of Indonesia.

Walk Facts

Start Merdeka Square (Monas)

End Ministry of Finance Building (Istiqlal)

Length 4.5km; two hours

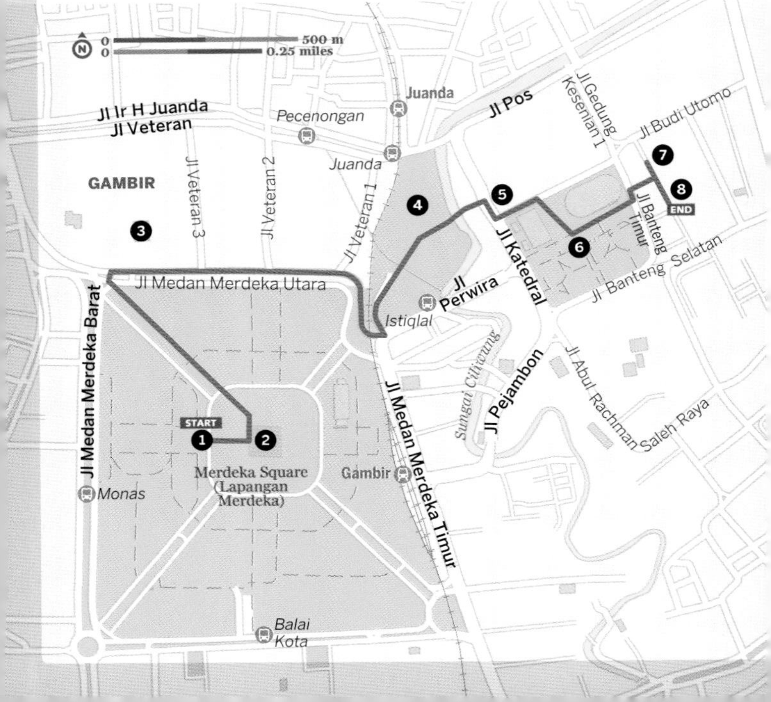

❶ Merdeka Square

Take a break from the frenetic pace of Jakarta with a stroll around Merdeka Square (p64). It's actually a trapezoid measuring almost 1 sq km that, in the 19th century, the Dutch called it Koningsplein (Kings Square).

❷ Monumen Nasional

Anchoring the square is the 132m-high Monumen Nasional (p65), constructed from Italian marble and topped with a sculpted flame that is gilded with 50kg of gold leaf. Enter the monument via an underground tunnel below the huge terrace.

❸ Istana Merdeka

Exit the square to the northwest, cross over Jl Medan Merdeka Utara and turn eastwards along the stout fence. The presidential palace (p72) was built in 1879 and was Sukarno's official residence during his presidency.

❹ Masjid Istiqlal

Continue walking east. Cross over Jl Veteran I and enter the grounds of Masjid Istiqlal (p72), Indonesia's national mosque. The building is striking and modernist, highlighted by geometrically grated windows.

❺ Gereja Katedral Jakarta

Exit the mosque grounds to the east over the canal and cross Jl Katedral to this Catholic cathedral (p73) with 60m-tall steeples and stained glass. It was built in 1901.

❻ Lapangan Banteng

Cross Jl Katedral along the south side of Gereja Katerdral Jakarta and walk to the middle of this square (p74), which is surrounded by some of Jakarta's best colonial architecture. Built by the Dutch in the early 19th century, it was originally called Waterlooplein.

❼ Mahkamah Agung

Walk to the east end of the square, and turn north on Jl Banteng Timur until you see the 1848 palace (p74) of the Dutch governor-general.

❽ Ministry of Finance Building

Head south for 200m. Next to the old Supreme Court is the grand Ministry of Finance Building (p74), which was the administrative centre for the Dutch government.

Map labels

A **B** **C** **D**

1

Jl Hayam Wuruk
Jl Gajah Mada
Jl Batu Ceper Raya
Jl Batu Tulis Raya
✗13
Jl Ceylan

Harmoni Central

2

Jl Ir H Juanda
Jl Veteran
Juanda
Pecenongan
✗14
Juanda

Jl Suryo Pranoto

Jl Medan Merdeka Utara

GAMBIR

Jl Veteran 3

Jl Pecenongan

Istana Merdeka
2

Jl Veteran 1

4 ⊙ Masji Istiqla

3

Jl Tanah Abang 1

Jl Medan Merdeka Utara

Istiqlal

Merdeka Square
⊙

Jl Medan Merdeka Barat

Jl Medan Merdeka Ti

Gambir 1

4

Jl Tanah Abang 2
Jl Abdul Muis

Monumen Nasional

Gambir

Jl Tanah Abang 4

⊙ Museum Nasional
Monas

Merdeka Square
(Lapangan Merdeka)

5

Jl Tanah Abang Timur

Arjuna Wijaya Statue **5** ⊙

Gambir 2

12 ✗

Jl Budi Kemuliaan

Balaikota
Jl Merdeka Selatan

6

Bank Indonesia

Jl Thamrin

Jl Agus Salim (Jl Sabang)

MENTENG

Jl Kebon Sirih Raya

A **B** **C** **D**

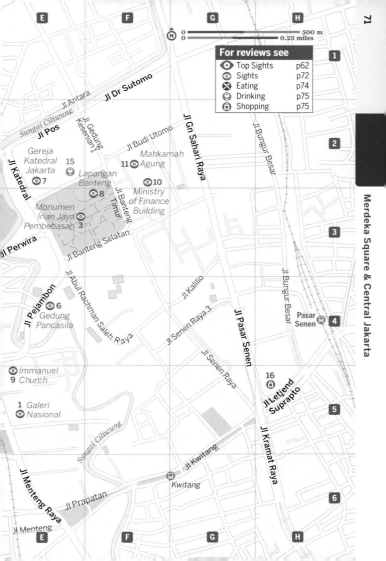

For reviews see

Top Sights	p62
Sights	p72
Eating	p74
Drinking	p75
Shopping	p75

Jl Antara

Jl Dr Sutomo

Sungai Ciliwung

Jl Pos

Jl Gedung Kesenian 1

Jl Budi Utomo

Jl Gn Sahari Raya

Jl Bungur Besar

Gereja Katedral Jakarta 15

7

Mahkamah 11 Agung

Lapangan Banteng

8

10

Ministry of Finance Building

Jl Katedral

Monumen Irian Jaya Pembebasan 3

Jl Banteng Timur

Jl Perwira

Jl Banteng Selatan

Jl Abdul Rachman Saleh Raya

Jl Kalilio

Jl Bungur Besar

Jl Pejambon

6

Gedung Pancasila

Jl Senen Raya 3

Jl Pasar Senen

Pasar Senen 4

Immanuel Church 9

Jl Senen Raya

16

1 Galeri Nasional

Jl Letjend Suprapto

Sungai Ciliwung

Jl Kramat Raya

Jl Menteng Raya

Jl Kwitang

Kwitang

Jl Prapatan

Jl Menteng

Sights

Galeri Nasional
GALLERY

1 MAP P70, E5

Over 1700 works of art by foreign and Indonesian artists are part of the National Gallery collection, which opened in 1999. Only a few works are on display at any time, but there are large spaces for regular – and well-curated – special exhibits. The centrepiece of the sprawling palm-shaded complex is an 1817 Dutch building. There's a small open-air cafe that offers a wonderful respite from pounding the local pavement pondering monuments. Visitors must check their bags into a cloakroom. (National Gallery; ☎021-3483 3954; http://galeri-nasional.or.id; Jl Medan Merdeka Timur 14; free; ☺9am-4pm Tue-Sun)

Istana Merdeka
PALACE

2 MAP P70, B3

The presidential palace (one of six in Indonesia) stands to the north of Merdeka Square. It was built in 1879 and was Sukarno's official residence during his presidency, although Suharto spurned it. On 27 December 1949, the Dutch flag was lowered for the last time and the red-and-white flag of independent Indonesia was raised. Hundreds of thousands of Indonesians gathered to witness the event and chant *merdeka* (freedom).

Every 17 August, Independence Day is celebrated with a flag-raising ceremony in front of the palace with thousands of dignitaries present. (Independence Palace; Jl Medan Merdeka Utara)

Monumen Irian Jaya Pembebasan
MONUMENT

3 MAP P70, E3

The twin towers of this monument with a dodgy provenance soar over grassy Lapangan Banteng (p74) and are topped by a sculpture of a man breaking his chains. It dates from the Sukarno era and was designed as anti-Imperialist propaganda, even as Indonesia annexed Irian Jaya (Timor and Papua) in 1963 despite local protests. These days some call it the 'Freedom Monument'. (Irian Jaya Liberation Monument; Lapangan Banteng)

Masjid Istiqlal
MOSQUE

4 MAP P70, D3

The striking, modernist Mesjid Istiqlal is adorned by patterned geometric grates on the windows. Completed in 1978, it's the largest mosque in Southeast Asia, with five levels representing the five pillars of Islam. Its dome is 45m across and its minaret tops 90m. Non-Muslim visitors are welcome. You have to sign in first and robe up (men should cover their legs, women their legs and arms). Once suitably dressed you'll be directed to a gallery overlooking the main hall.

During Ramadan more than 200,000 worshippers can be accommodated here. The building was designed by Catholic architect Frederich Silaban. (Independence Mosque: Jl Veteran I; free; ⏰4am-11pm)

Arjuna Wijaya Statue
MONUMENT

5 ◉ MAP P70, B5

Built in 1987, this enormous statue near a major road junction depicts the Hindu hero Arjuna in his chariot pulled by eight horses. (Jl Medan Merdeka Barat)

Gedung Pancasila
HISTORIC BUILDING

6 ◉ MAP P70, E4

Gedung Pancasila is an imposing neoclassical building built in 1830 as the Dutch army commander's residence. It later became the meeting hall of the Volksraad (People's Council), but is best known as the place where Sukarno made his famous Pancasila speech on 18 August 1945, laying the foundation for Indonesia's constitution. It's now part of the Ministry of Foreign Affairs. (Jl Pejambon)

Gereja Katedral Jakarta
CHURCH

7 ◉ MAP P70, E2

This Roman Catholic cathedral has an impressive height, with lacy twin spires made from wrought iron, each 60m tall. It was built in 1901 to replace an earlier church. Look for stained-glass features. At the time of research, a small museum about the sight was under renovation. (Jakarta Cathedral; 📞021-351 9186; Jl Katedral 7B; ⏰5am-9pm)

Masjid Istiqlal

Independence Day in Merdeka Square

If you're anywhere near Jakarta on Indonesia's Independence Day, and don't mind crowds, head for the north side of Merdeka Square and witness all the pomp the nation's ruling elite can muster during morning celebrations in front of Istana Merdeka.

Lapangan Banteng SQUARE

8 MAP P70, F3

Just east of Merdeka Square is Lapangan Banteng, which is surrounded by some of Jakarta's best colonial architecture. It was first designed by the Dutch in the early 19th century, when it was called Waterlooplein.

It has basketball courts, football pitches and a children's play area. (Banteng Sq; btwn Jl Banteng Timur & Jl Katedral)

Immanuel Church CHURCH

9 ⊙ MAP P70, E5

This classic church dates from 1834. The interior is smaller than you'd think, but it has a round dome and an organ dating from 1843.

Ask to see the church at the gate and tip the guard for letting you in. (📞 021-344 0747; http://gpibimmanueljakarta.org; Jl Medan Merdeka Timur 10; ⊙8am-5pm)

Ministry of Finance Building HISTORIC BUILDING

10 ⊙ MAP P70, F2

Next door to the 1848 columned old Supreme Court is the Ministry of Finance Building, formerly the Witte Huis (White House). This grand complex was built by Dutch Governor-General Hermann Willem Daendels in 1809 as the administrative centre for the Dutch government. (Departemen Bangunan Keuangan; Jl Banteng Timur 1)

Mahkamah Agung NOTABLE BUILDING

11 ⊙ MAP P70, F2

Part of the Ministry of Finance complex, this grand columned edifice with a deep portico was the colonial-era palace of the Daendels. It was built in 1848. (Former Supreme Court; Jl Banteng Timur)

Eating

Lenggang Jakarta INDONESIAN $

12 ✖ MAP P70, B5

One of Merdeka Square's best features is this well-organised assortment of food stalls. Sample foods from across the archipelago from more than 50 cheap-and-cheerful vendors. Order everything from spicy noodle dishes (chicken, fish and veggie) from East Java to Indonesian omelettes, cooked in a hot wok in front of you. Enjoy the bounty at long communal tables. (www.lenggangjakarta.com; Merdeka Sq; mains from 20,000Rp; ⊙10am-11pm)

Lulu & Kayla Cakes

CAFE $

13 📍 MAP P70, C1

Éclairs, cupcakes, croissants and other irresistible goodies are baked on-site at this cute mint-green stand-alone cafe. Cakes are beautifully presented with heaped cream and sprinkles, and are made using fine ingredients like Belgian chocolate. Choose from melt-in-the-mouth red velvet, Baileys, coffee, carrot, white-chocolate almond and Nutella cupcakes, then wash them down with the house hot chocolate.

Savoury snacks like fries and onion rings also available. (📞021-384 5777; Jl Batu Tulis Raya 50; cupcakes from 35,000Rp; ⏰8am-8pm)

Restoran Sari Minang

INDONESIAN $

14 📍 MAP P70, D2

The veteran waiters at this Padang-style eatery have been serving diners since 1968. It's cafeteria style with faded red chairs and fluorescent lighting, but it's immensely popular. Try the spicy curries and cool off in the air-con. (📞021-3483 4524; Jl Ir H Juanda 4; mains 20,000-50,000Rp; ⏰8am-midnight; ❄)

Drinking

Filateli Coffee

CAFE

15 🚇 MAP P70, E2

This very small, simple cafe next to the **main post office** (⏰7.30am-7pm Mon-Fri, to 1pm Sat) is handy if you're in need of a pick-me-up while exploring Jakarta's big squares. It serves manual brews, juices, teas and snacks like croissants, French fries and simple noodle dishes (from 23,500Rp). (📞0812 237 1314; Jl Katedral 1; coffee from 20,000Rp; ⏰7am-8pm Mon-Fri, to 1pm Sat)

Shopping

Pasar Senen Jaya

MALL

16 🔒 MAP P70, H5

The mall for the masses, this huge complex has myriad shops and vendors selling just about every day-to-day item imaginable. Cheap shoes, batik clothes, homewares, toys – the list goes on and on. In the mornings, throngs of bakers on the southeast side sell fresh sweets. (📞021-422 2525; Jl Pasar Senen; ⏰7am-5pm)

Explore ◈
Cikini & Menteng

South of Merdeka Square, the adjoining neighbour-hoods of Cikini and Menteng are Jakarta at its genteel best. Many streets are tree-lined and even the canals seem relatively clean. Cikini's main drag, Jl Cikini Raya, is lined with good cafes and restaurants. Menteng has Jakarta's commercial spine, the major road of Jl Thamrin, and its top-end hotels and malls.

The Short List

○ **Plaza Indonesia (p94)** *Discover exquisite goods from near and far at this grand shopping mall and others like it in the area.*

○ **Kunstkring Paleis (p85)** *Savour the best of Indonesian cuisine.*

○ **Taman Suropati (p82)** *Sense the languid charms of Jakarta's past in the streets around this park.*

○ **Pasar Jl Surabaya (p94)** *Browse through hundreds of stalls for treasures real and fake at this vibrant street market.*

○ **Cloud Lounge (p89)** *Sip a cocktail high above the smog at this 49th-floor open-air bar.*

Getting There & Around

🚌 Several routes on the Transjakarta run along Jl Thamrin.

🚕 Just south of Jakarta's traditional centre, Cikini and Menteng are easily reached by taxi from all corners of the city.

🚆 When traffic is bad, the train is a good option for getting to Soekarno-Hatta International Airport (70,000Rp, 45 minutes).

Neighbourhood Map on p80

Walking Tour 🥾

Jakarta's Revolutionary Heart

Today the quieter streets of Menteng are tree-lined retreats for the city's upper classes. Stylish homes built with curvaceous art-deco lines date from colonial times before WWII. This was the heart of Indonesia's independence movement, which grew in the salons of its educated residents. You can still find sites linked to these times today.

Walk Facts

Start Taman Suporati
(🚇 Cikini)
End Camden Bar
(🚇 Cikini)
Length 2km; one hour

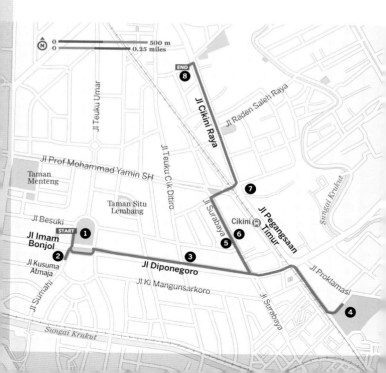

❶ Taman Suropati

This park (p82) dotted with modern statues is a surprising patch of green amid the city traffic. It's at the heart of a preservation zone for colonial bungalows, many of which qualify as mansions with art-deco touches that flourished in Java in the 1920s.

❷ Museum Perumusan Naskah Proklamasi

Once a mansion (p82), this museum now commemorates the building's role in Indonesia's independence at the end of WWII. It was the home of the Japanese naval commander Tadashi Maeda and is where, on 16 August 1945, Sukarno and Hatta were convinced the time had come to compose the proclamation that was announced the following day.

❸ Adam Malik House

Now looking shambolic, this art-deco house at Jl Diponegoro 29 was the home for many years of Adam Malik, who played a critical role in Indonesia's independence. On 16 August 1945, he led a group who kidnapped Sukarno and Hatta and demanded they stop dithering and declare independence. The pair proceeded to do just that.

❹ Taman Proklamasi

The former home of Sukarno, from which Indonesian independence was proclaimed, stood on the site of this large public square (p82). There is a monument, with large statues of President Sukarno and Vice-President Hatta, which was designed by Nyoman Nuarta, a famous Balinese artist.

❺ Cali Deli

Try the delicious banh mi (Vietnamese sandwiches) at this super-casual eatery (p88).

❻ Pasar Jl Surabaya

Visit this popular street market (p94) to browse busy stalls filled with everything from jewellery and clothing to furniture and antiques. Many of the vendors here are real characters, with their own line of patter. You'll be laughing by your third clever exchange.

❼ Cikini Gold Center

Whether you want a discreet necklace to add a little sparkle at the beach or some major bling to make a statement, this huge complex (p94) offers myriad shops that will help you find the perfect treasure.

❽ Camden Bar

Camden Bar (p90) is a fine place to relax after a walk. Grab a seat outdoors on the terrace and enjoy the well-priced beers and food from the bar.

1
2
3
4
5
6

A **B** **C** **D**

Jl KH Wahid Hasyim

Jl KH Wahid Hasyim

Jl Kebon Kacang 1

Sarinah

Jl Sunda

Jl Sumatera

Jl Thamrin

Jl Jaksa

Jl Kebon Sirih Timur

Jl Gereja Theresia

Jl Cokroaminoto

Jl Dr Sam

Kampung
Bali

Jl Kebon Kacang 11

Jl Kebon Kacang 9

Jl Thamrin

Jl Agus Salim (Jl Sabang)

Jl Jusuf Adiwinata

Jl Maluku

Jl Lombok

Jl Tanjung

Bundaran
HI

39 🚇 📍 26
27 📍

9 ❌

Jl Suwiryo

Jl Kebon Kacang Raya

25 ☕

34 ❌ 24 ❌ 16
19 ❌ ☆ 36
18 ☆ 6
Energy
Reflexology
Bar

40 📍
23 ❌

📍 4
Welcome
Monument

Jl Prof Mohammad Yamin SH

13 ❌

Jl Sultan Syahrir

Taman
Menteng

17 ❌
📍 32
33

38 🔒

Jl Cokroaminoto

Jl Sidorajo

12 ❌

Tosari
ICBC 🚇

Jl Imam Bonjol

Jl Kusuma Atmaja

Jl Besuki
SDN Menteng 1 📍
School 5

Jl Sumenep

Jl Imam Bonjol
Museum Perumusan
Naskah Proklamasi 1 📍

Taman
Lawang

Jl Kusuma Atmaja

Jl Sumahir

Jl Thamrin

Jl Kendal

Sudirman
Station 🚇

Jl Kendal

Sungai Krukut

🧭 N

0   500 m
0   0.25 miles

A **B** **C** **D**

For reviews see

⊙	Sights	p82
✕	Eating	p84
🍷	Drinking	p89
✿	Entertainment	p92
🔒	Shopping	p94

Sights

Museum Perumusan Naskah Proklamasi

MUSEUM

1 ◉ MAP P80, D5

This atmospheric mansion saw historic events as Indonesia proclaimed its independence at the end of WWII. It was the home of the Japanese naval commander Tadashi Maeda and is where, on 16 August 1945, Sukarno and Hatta were convinced the time had come to compose the proclamation that was announced the following day. The museum features the meeting room of those present that night and includes details like the typewriter where the words were pounded out.

A brief message to the world, the proclamation was forced by youth groups, notably the Menteng 31 Asrama (whose leader Adam Malik later had a house down the street at Jl Diponegoro 29). They 'kidnapped' Sukarno and Hatta and forced them to stop dithering and declare independence. The final draft was worked out with the assistance of Admiral Maeda, who had always been sympathetic to the independence movement and helped the cause as the Japanese waited to surrender to Allied forces. (📞021-314 4743; http://munasprok. or.id; Jl Imam Bonjol 1; adult/child 2000/1000Rp; ⏰8am-4pm Tue-Thu, 8-11.30am & 1-4.30pm Fri, 8.30am-4pm Sat & Sun)

Taman Suropati

PLAZA

2 ◉ MAP P80, E5

A village green surrounded by mansions, this area is a preservation zone for the colonial bungalows. Many really qualify as mansions and have the art-deco touches that flourished in Java in the 1920s. The park itself is a surprising patch of greenery amid the traffic. It is dotted with modern statuary that has been gifted by other Asian governments. There's also a dovecote and lots of roaming cats among the art pieces. (Jl Iman Bonjol & Jl Teuku Umar)

Taman Proklamasi

SQUARE

3 ◉ MAP P80, H5

Indonesia's independence was proclaimed on 17 August 1945 at the former home of Sukarno, which stood on the site of this large public square at Jl Proklamasi 56 (it was later done in by poor maintenance). The imposing monument, with large statues of President Sukarno and Vice-President Hatta, was designed by Nyoman Nuarta, a famous Balinese artist. The proclamation text is carved into a black marble cube. Other monuments honour various aspects of the revolution. (Jl Proklamasi)

Jakarta Planetarium & Observatory

PLANETARIUM

Travel the galaxy in only an hour at this popular planetarium that's part of the Taman Ismail Marzuki (see 35 ✪ Map p80, G2, p92) cultural complex.

There are two to four shows each day, suitable for families. (☎021-230 5146; http://planetarium.jakarta.go.id; Jl Cikini Raya 73; adult/child 12,000/7000Rp; ⏱8am-3.30pm Mon-Fri, 7am-4pm Sat & Sun; 🚼)

Welcome Monument MONUMENT

4 ◉ MAP P80, B4

Set in the centre of a fountain on one of central Jakarta's most prominent *alun-aluns* (public squares) is the Salamat Datang, or Welcome Monument. Built in 1962, it's just across from the **Hotel Indonesia Kempinski** (☎021-2358 3800; www.kempinski.com), the city's original luxury hotel. At the very top of the monument is a man and a woman, each with an arm up waving a warm welcome. (Salamat Datang; Jl Thamrin)

SDN Menteng 1 School NOTABLE BUILDING

5 ◉ MAP P80, D5

Barack Obama attended this government-run primary school from 1969 to 1971. It's in a fairly posh neighbourhood and is known as the school of choice for many of Jakarta's business and government elite. There's a plaque recalling his attendance near the entrance, plus a statue of him as a boy. (Jl Besuki)

Energy Reflexology Bar MASSAGE

6 ◉ MAP P80, A4

Provides an excellent express reflexology foot massage for those tired from shopping all day. Other massages (back, neck and

Welcome Monument

Cikini & Menteng Sights

In the Shadow of Luxury: Kampung Bali

Literally in the shadow of the rarefied high-end world of the Grand Indonesia and Plaza Indonesia malls, **Kampung Bali** (Map p80, A2; off Jl Kebon Kacang Raya) is typical of where most middle-class Jakartans live. Follow the narrow streets and lanes at random (all are named 'Jl Kebon Kacang' followed by a number). Shops selling all manner of mundane items like produce and plastic buckets are mixed with homes – some compact and single-family, others even more compact and multi-family.

You'll also find repair shops and stalls selling quick bites to eat to the ever-frenetic locals. Look for signs saying 'Kost Wanita', which are supervised dorms for young single women who come to Jakarta from rural villages to earn money and possibly find a better life. Inscrutable house mothers ensure that life (at least inside the dorm) remains chaste and help to reassure nervous relatives back home.

shoulder) are also available, but aren't as effective – they're done on reclining chairs rather than on massage beds. There's another location in Kota. (☑021-2358 0606; 3rd fl, Grand Indonesia Mall East, Jl Thamrin; 30min foot massage from 120,000Rp; ☉10am-10pm)

Cikini Swimming Pool

SWIMMING

7 ◉ MAP P80, G3

Hidden behind the Ibis Budget Hotel Cikini (p140) is a public Olympic-sized swimming pool. Surrounded by cafes, it's not the most private of locations, but is a decent place for a workout nevertheless. (☑021-3190 0588; Jl Cikini Raya 75; Mon-Fri 40,000Rp, Sat & Sun 50,000Rp; ☉8am-8pm Mon-Fri, 7am-11pm Sat, 7am-8pm Sun)

Eating

Gado Gado Bon Bin

INDONESIAN $

8 ✖ MAP P80, G3

A much-loved, open-fronted, no-frills outlet for simple Indonesian dishes, Bon Bin has been stir-frying up classics for over 50 years. The namesake gado gado is always fresh, with silky peanut sauce. Everything is bare-bones but the flavour. (☑021-392 5404; Jl Cikini 4; mains 25,000-35,000Rp; ☉10am-5pm)

Plataran Menteng

INDONESIAN $$

9 ✖ MAP P80, D3

This excellent restaurant in a grand, old, light-and-airy mansion has plenty of ambience. There's a live pianist, birdcages and reminders of a bygone era, but it's not stuffy or pretentious. Asian fusion with Indonesian flavours is done well. Try the nasi goreng four ways, pad thai, shrimp vermicelli, grilled chicken skewers, or roasted duck with mangosteen and curry sauce. (☑021-2962 7771; www.plataran.com; Jl Cokroaminoto 42; ⊙11am-10pm)

Tjikini INDONESIAN $$

10 ✖ MAP P80, F2

On one of the best coffee strips in Jakarta, this appealing cafe has an alluring vintage style with bentwood chairs and tiled floors. Coffee drinks are superb; the menu has creative takes on Indonesian fare and flavoursome noodles. (☑021-3193 5521; http://tjikini.com; Jl Cikini Raya 17; mains 55,000-190,000Rp; ⊙7am-11pm; 🛜)

Kunstkring Paleis INDONESIAN $$

11 ✖ MAP P80, E2

High tea or cocktails? You can have both, plus a divine Indonesian dinner in between at this alluring re-imagined Dutch colonial mansion, once Batavia's fine arts centre (it showed works by Van Gogh, Picasso, Chagall and Gauguin after it opened in 1914), where exhibitions continue today. The main Pangeran Diponegoro Room, with its wall-sized canvases, is where you'll have traditional tea service with an Indonesian twist. Cultural dances sometimes take place during dinner service (ask your waitstaff). Or come a bit later and enjoy a drink in the red-lit Susie Wong lounge, named after the infamous Hong Kong madame. There's also a wine

shop on-site. (☑021-390 0899; www.tuguhotels.com; Jl Teuku Umar 1; mains 68,000-488,000Rp; ⊙5pm-midnight)

Maple & Oak INTERNATIONAL $$

12 ✖ MAP P80, D4

With modern, Scandi-esque design, incorporating pastel tones and plants in terrariums, this cute spot around the corner from Barack Obama's old school serves delicious salads and all-day brunch, ranging from hazelnut chocolate toast to seared Norwegian salmon. Smoothies and coffees too (including cold brews). (☑021-390 6757; http://mapleandoakjkt.com; Jl Cokroaminoto 91; mains 68,000-98,000Rp; ⊙8am-9pm)

Seribu Rasa Menteng INDONESIAN $$

13 ✖ MAP P80, C4

An excellent low-key local chain restaurant just a short walk from glitzy malls and hotels. Classic Indonesian dishes from satay to beef rendang are served along with fine fresh seafood in a relaxed colonial-style room. Look for influences from other Asian nations. Drink Heineken on tap. (☑021-392 8892; http://arenacorp.com/seribu-rasa; Jl Haji Agus Salim 128; dishes 62,000-160,000Rp; ⊙11am-3pm & 6-10pm Mon-Thu, 11am-10pm Fri-Sun)

Warung Daun INDONESIAN $$

14 ✖ MAP P80, G2

This re-imagined warung (food stall) attempts a modern and

healthy take on classic dishes. Expect delectable Sundanese and Chinese Indonesian dishes, prepared using organic ingredients whenever possible, and presented tastefully. Wash them down with an array of fruit drinks. It's set in an atmospheric old green-and-white painted house set back from the street. (✆021-391 0909; www. warungdaun.com; Jl Cikini 26; mains 27,000-110,000Rp; ⏰10am-11pm)

Lara Djonggrang INDONESIAN $$

15 ✖ MAP P80, F3

It's easy to think you've stumbled across an enchanting lost temple at Lara Djonggrang. Its dimly lit, incense-filled space is decorated with traditional furnishings – dark-wood chairs, red tablecloths and Indonesian sculptures and art. Imperial Indonesian dishes are tasty and beautifully presented. Interestingly, the bar was actually created from part of a 200-year-old temple.

Dishes range from Makassar-style squid and crab to Alor-style tamarind shrimp, and lobster cooked Aceh-style. There's a good wine list and staff are well informed and efficient. Prices are affordable considering the quality. Service can be slow when the dining room is busy. (✆021-315 3252; www.tugu hotels.com; Jl Teuku Cik Ditiro 4; mains 80,000-130,000Rp; ⏰11am-1am; 🛜)

Seven Friday INTERNATIONAL $$

16 ✖ MAP P80, A4

Good brunch spot in a trendy retro space with a display of vintage phones and radios and a polished factory chic feel. You can't go wrong with the croque madame or eggs Bennie before 4pm. For dinner, the pork chop rice is insanely good – it's served with crispy sambal matah (spicy shallot salsa), fragrant rice and a spicy aromatic broth. (✆021-2992 4380; www.facebook. com/sevenfridayspace; level 2, Plaza Indonesia, Jl Thamrin 28-30; mains 47,000-207,000Rp; ⏰10am-10pm)

Publik Markette INTERNATIONAL $$

17 ✖ MAP P80, B4

A funky spot with geometric lamp-shades, bright colours, solid marble counter tops and patterned chairs, serving a mixture of Asian and Western eats. Order dishes like butter chicken, Balinese sambal sea bass and oxtail fried rice, plus pizzas, pastas and salads. Smoothie bowls are a good start to the day, and there's buy-one-get-one-free coffee (9am to 11am). (✆021-2358 1281; www.facebook. com/PublikMarkette; ground fl, Grand Indonesia East Mall, Jl Thamrin 1; mains 85,000-230,000Rp; ⏰10am-11pm Sun-Thu, to midnight Fri & Sat)

Social House BREAKFAST $$

18 ✖ MAP P80, A4

This open-plan space at Grand Indonesia (p94) mall has an attached wine shop. Diners can enjoy a courtyard feel (and indoor trees!). It serves dinner, but the Western breakfast options are particularly good – including granola and avocado tartines, smoked salmon bagels, Spanish omelettes and Wagyu beef hash, plus shakshuka. (☎ 021-2358 1818; www.ismaya.com/eat-drink/social-house; level 1, Grand Indonesia East Mall, Jl Thamrin 1; dishes 95,000-135,000Rp; ☺8am-1am)

Union INTERNATIONAL $$

19 MAP P80, A4

A small Indonesian chain inspired by New York; the decor is French brasserie meets art deco. It has a bakery selling fresh loaves and sourdough, plus a dining room, with red couches, serving fennel-crusted pork belly and crispy skinned salmon, plus pasta and burgers. Also serves coffee. (☎ 021-2358 0476; www.unionjkt.com; ground fl, Lobby Shinta, Grand Indonesia East Mall, Jl Thamrin 1; mains 95,000-170,000Rp; ☺10am-10pm)

Diyar MIDDLE EASTERN $$

20 MAP P80, F2

Arabian themed with pretty floor tiles, this Middle Eastern restaurant has a large menu of more than 100 dishes – everything from kebabs and felafel to fattoush and tabbouleh salads, plus some rather good meat and rice dishes. (☎ 021-391 5893, 0858 8810 0051; Jl Cikini Raya 33; dishes 50,000-420,000Rp; ☺9am-11pm; ☂)

Dua Nyonya INDONESIAN $$

Also a cafe, Dua Nyonya (see 20 Map p80, F2) is an intimate place serving fine Indonesian coffee (from Bali, Toraja and Aceh) and traditional food including rice dishes, such as *nasi bebek goreng keramat* (fried rice with duck).

Cikini & Menteng Eating

Nasi bebek goreng keramat

Classical music and art add to the ambience. (☎021-314 4691; Jl Cikini Raya 27; dishes 45,000-110,000Rp; ☻7am-midnight; 🛜)

Tjikinii Lima Restaurant & Cafe
INTERNATIONAL $$

21 ❌ MAP P80, F2

A pretty courtyard setting with a restaurant serving fish and chips, flatbreads and sandwiches, and simple Asian plates of chicken with rice or noodles. Unusual dishes include 'mac and chick' (macaroni cheese with fried chicken). (☎021-390 0745; Jl Cikini I 5; mains 48,000-120,000Rp; ☻10am-10pm Sun-Thu, to midnight Fri & Sat)

Cali Deli
DELI $$

22 ❌ MAP P80, G5

A super-casual place for sandwiches right across from Pasar Jl Surabaya (p94). Prowl the market looking for an actual genuine antique, then enjoy soup in a bread bowl in the tidy dining room. It adjoins Madame Ching, which serves Vietnamese mains. You can order from either menu. (☎021-315 0363, 021-392 5364; Jl Surabaya 22; mains 50,000-75,000Rp; ☻10am-10pm; 🛜)

OKU
JAPANESE $$$

23 ❌ MAP P80, B4

Inside Hotel Indonesia Kempinski (p83), OKU is an outstanding Japanese dining experience. Its Zen-like minimalist dining room allows the food to stand out. Chef Kazumasa Yazawa serves up modernised Japanese cuisine, but don't mistake this for fusion. Standout dishes include the extraordinary Wagyu with macadamia nuts and black garlic miso, Japanese hot pot and sashimi cuts. Reservations recommended. (☎021-2358 3896; www.kempinski.com; Hotel Indonesia Kempinski, Jl Thamrin; mains 140,000-1,350,000Rp; ☻noon-3pm & 6-10.30pm; 🛜)

Por Que No
TAPAS $$$

A tucked-away, uberhip rooftop tapas bar with terrace in the De Ritz Building in Menteng (see 12 ❌ Map p80, D4), this spot is popular with those in the know. Try the grilled and sliced tenderloin, deep-fried dory, mozzarella balls, calamari in its own ink and prawns sautéed with chilli and garlic. Best to save room for a dessert of churro ice-cream sandwiches. (☎021-390 1950; http://porqueno.co.id; 5th fl, Jl Cokroaminoto 91; dishes 45,000-260,000Rp; ☻noon-midnight Tue-Thu & Sun, to 2am Fri & Sat; 🛜)

Crystal Jade Palace
CHINESE $$$

24 ❌ MAP P80, A4

Expand your culinary palate at this branch of the acclaimed Michelin-starred Singapore chain, located at Grand Indonesia (p94) mall. The high-end Chinese dining experience includes exceptional quality and authentic regional Chinese dishes. You won't find sweet and sour chicken here: instead the roasted Peking duck is out of this world and the soupy crab *xiao long bao* dumplings are delicious.

Adventurous eaters can try braised abalone, fish maw or sea cucumber. Stay away from the shark fin soup (eating endangered animals is not cool). (☎021-2358 0768; www.crystaljade.com; upper ground level, Grand Indonesia Mall, Jl Thamrin 1; dishes 128,000-820,000Rp; ⏱11am-2.30pm & 6-9.30pm Mon-Fri, 10.30am-2.30pm & 6-9.30pm Sat & Sun)

Drinking

Tanamera Coffee COFFEE

25 MAP P80, A3

A real contender for Jakarta's best cup of coffee is this third-wave roaster that offers a range of single-origin beans from around Indonesia. It now has numerous branches, but this is the original, and is where it roasts its beans.

Coffee is prepared either as V60 pour-overs or by espresso machine, along with tasty breakfasts. Try dishes such as citrus and creamy eggs Benedict, croque madame or soft-shell crab burgers. Find it in an unlikely backstreet next to Thamrin City shopping centre. (☎021-2962 5599; www.tanameracoffee.com; Jl Kebon Kacang Raya Blok AA07; coffee from 30,000Rp; ⏱7am-6.30pm; ☎)

Immigrant CLUB

26 MAP P80, B3

By day this is a stylish art-deco dining lounge high atop the trendy Plaza Indonesia (p94) mall. At night, the adjacent club serves crafted cocktails and imported wines and hosts top DJs (who mix R&B, hip-hop and bubblegum rock). It attracts a glamorous local and expat crowd. Happy hour runs from 4pm to 10pm with 25% off selected drinks.

The dining room serves dishes like slow-cooked lamb, pork chop with parsnip purée, and pizza. Small plates such as chicken wings, fries and calamari are available from the bar when the main dining area is closed. (☎021-2992 4126; www.immigrant-jakarta.com; 6th fl, Plaza Indonesia, Jl Thamrin 28-30; mains from 80,000Rp, cover varies; ⏱11am-1am Sun-Tue, to 4am Wed-Sat)

Cloud Lounge LOUNGE

27 MAP P80, B3

Gourmet bites in a decadent dining room, flaming cocktails, an indoor-outdoor lounge with views of the entire city from the 49th floor of the Plaza tower – this hip spot is a mainstay on Jakarta's up-market night scene. Meals range from pasta and rice dishes to Wagyu rib-eye. While 360-degree views are lure enough, there are also rotating DJs. (☎021-2992 2450; www.cloudjakarta.com; 49th fl, The Plaza, Jl Thamrin; mains from 130,000Rp, cover varies; ⏱dining 6.30-11pm, lounge 4pm-2am Sun-Thu, to 3am Fri & Sat)

Bakoel Koffie

CAFE

28 MAP P80, F1

Occupying a fine old colonial building dating from 1878, this elegant art-deco-style cafe has twirling ceiling fans, marble-top round tables and vintage weighing scales and clocks. It serves strong coffee using beans from across the archipelago. Cakes, breakfasts and local dishes like nasi goreng and *bubur ayam* (Jakarta-style chicken with spicy peanut sauce) can also be ordered. (www.bakoelkoffie.com; Jl Cikini Raya 25; dishes 30,000-70,000Rp; 9am-midnight Mon, 8am-midnight Tue-Sun;)

Camden Bar

BAR

29 MAP P80, F2

Behind the bland wall facing a side street, this bar is a fine place to re-treat for an evening. You can chill in the woodsy air-con lounge or take in the air outside on the terrace. Beer prices are good and there's a wide range of cocktails, plus bourbon and single malt whiskies, and a range of bar food. (021-310 1283; Jl Cikini Raya 2; 5am-2am;)

Goeboex Coffee

COFFEE

30 MAP P80, G2

This industrial-style hang-out built from metal containers as an upper terrace from where to watch the goings-on of Jl Cikini Raya. It serves single-origin brews and manual pours. A small food menu includes local and Western dishes like nasi goreng, fish and chips and red-hot chilli chicken. (Jl Cikini I 57A; coffee from 25,000Rp, dishes 25,000-35,000Rp; 11am-2am)

Waitstaff at Bakoel Koffie

Barack Obama's Jakarta Connections

Former US president Barack Obama lived in Jakarta for four years as a child. This was a source of great pride to Indonesians during his presidency and also served his political enemies, who claimed that he attended a fundamentalist Islamic school. The reality is actually much different.

Obama moved to Jakarta in 1967, when he was six years old, following his mother's marriage to Lolo Soetoro, an Indonesian geographer; the couple met while studying at the University of Hawaii.

Young Barack initially attended Santo Fransiskus Asisi, a Roman Catholic school near his home in the Kuningan area south of the city. After nearly three years being taught by the reportedly demanding priests, Barack and his family moved north to the more up-market neighbourhood of Menteng.

For the remaining year and a half before they left Jakarta in 1971, Barack attended SDN Menteng 1 (p83), a government-run school, which now has a plaque and statue dedicated to him. A popular child, he was nicknamed 'Barry' by his fellow students. It's even been reported that he declared an ambition to become the US president while at this school. The family lived close by on Jl Taman Amir Hamzah, in a handsome terracotta-tiled Dutch villa with art-deco-style windows.

All this would have been forgotten if his time in Jakarta hadn't become an issue exploited by his political opponents. Throughout Obama's presidency, conservative American politicians portrayed SDN Menteng 1 as a 'Madrassa' school where the young Barack was indoctrinated with some form of fundamentalism. The irony is that this couldn't be less true as Basuki (as it's known) is actually the school of choice for the children of Jakarta's largely secular business and government elites.

Indeed, these are the same people who have used their power to firmly tie Obama to Basuki as a point of pride. Meanwhile, the Asisi school, where he spent the bulk of his time, was written out of the narrative, although staff there have erected a plaque to honour their own ties to Obama.

Workroom Coffee COFFEE

31 MAP P80, F1

Workroom Coffee has Scandi-like modern interiors set up for co-working; there are plenty of single spaces for those wanting to use their laptop. The food menu includes Asian rice bowls and snacks, plus Western plates such as chicken cordon bleu and fish and chips. (0881 164 1514; www.facebook.com/workroomcoffee; Jl Cikini Raya 9; menu items 35,000-45,000Rp; 10am-10pm, to 8pm Sun;)

Paulaner Bräuhaus PUB

32 MAP P80, B4

In a country not known for its diversity of beer options, this German-themed pub offers a point of difference with its house-brewed, unfiltered lager, dunkel and Weissbier wheat beer. There's a menu of hearty Bavarian cuisine, including pork products aplenty (knuckles, bacon or sausages) or just grab a freshly baked pretzel to enjoy while watching sport on the many TVs. (021-2358 3871; www.paulaner-brauhaus-worldwide.com; Grand Indonesia East Mall, Jl Thamrin 1; beer 300mL/500mL/1L 82,000/99,000/169,000Rp; menu items from 39,000Rp; 11.30am-midnight Sun-Thu, to 1am Fri & Sat)

Skye Bar & Restaurant LOUNGE

33 MAP P80, B4

Sit outside like an eagle at this eyrie in the sky. At the very top of one of Indonesia's biggest banks, you can lounge outside with the sweep of Jakarta before you, or have a slightly more discreet view from one of the sofas inside. Entry is 250,000Rp on weekends, which is redeemable for drinks and snacks at the bar. (021-2358 6996; www.facebook.com/skye.jakarta; 56th fl, BCA Tower, Jl Thamrin 1; beers/cocktails from 70,000/120,000Rp, menu items 95,000-345,000Rp; restaurant 5-11pm, bar 4pm-1am Sun-Thu, to 2am Fri & Sat)

Entertainment

CGV Grand Indonesia CINEMA

34 MAP P80, A4

If you've never had a VIP cinema experience, this is the place to do it. Gold class has a premium lounge, reclining chairs and waiter service (you can buy drinks and snacks from your chair), while velvet class has actual beds, which fit two people. The complex also has virtual-reality headset booths and regular screens. (021-2358 0484; www.cgv.id; level 8, Grand Indonesia West Mall, Jl Thamrin 1; regular tickets 50,000Rp, gold/velvet class from 100,000Rp/220,000Rp)

Taman Ismail Marzuki PERFORMING ARTS

35 MAP P80, G2

Jakarta's premier cultural centre has a great selection of cinemas, theatres and exhibition spaces. Performances (such as Sundanese dance and gamelan music events) are always high quality and the complex has a cafeteria too. Check the website for upcoming events. (TIM; ☏ 021-3193 7530, 021-230 5146; http://tamanismailmarzuki.jakarta. go.id; Jl Cikini Raya 73)

T-Rex Family Karaoke KARAOKE

36 ⭐ MAP P80, A4

Despite the name, this is not a particularly family-friendly place. Kids are welcome, but it can get pretty boozy. The dozens of private karaoke rooms range in size. You can order a selection of alcoholic drinks and food via waiter service. Songs range from western R&B and hip-hop to Chinese and K-pop hits. (☏ 021-2358 0855; www.t-rexktv. com; level 3, Grand Indonesia West Mall, Jl Thamrin 1; small room up to 4 people 1hr 93,000Rp; ⏱ noon-2.30am Mon-Fri, to 3am Sat, to 1am Sun)

Metropole XXI CINEMA

37 ⭐ MAP P80, H5

Housed in a historic theatre (the oldest in Jakarta), this plush cinema with gold trim is worth a visit. It shows Western movies in English. There's a restaurant, coffee shop and snack bar. (☏ 021-3192 2249; www.21cineplex.com; Jl Pegangsaan Tengah 21; tickets Mon-Thu 40,000Rp, Fri 50,000Rp, Sat & Sun 60,000Rp)

TIM XXI CINEMA

Next to the Taman Ismail Marzuki (see 35 ⭐ Map p80, G2) centre, this inexpensive movie theatre shows the latest Western blockbusters in English with Indonesian subtitles. (☏ 021-319 25130; www.21cineplex. com; Taman Ismail Marzuki, Jl Cikini Raya 73; tickets from 30,000Rp)

Taman Ismail Marzuki

Shopping

Bartele Gallery

MAPS

38 🏠 MAP P80, B4

On the 1st floor of the Mandarin Oriental Hotel, a treasure trove of antique maps awaits at this compact shop. Prints, some dating back 500 years, are also displayed. Look for originals drawn by explorers to document their discoveries. Photos from the 19th century and a smattering of antiques round out your visit. (📞021-2993 8997; www.bartele gallery.com; Mandarin Oriental Hotel, Jl Thamrin; ⏱11am-8pm)

Plaza Indonesia

MALL

39 🏠 MAP P80, B3

This high-end mall is centrally located and offers a wide selection of shops, including leading Indonesian boutiques and the likes of Cartier and Louis Vuitton. In the basement there's an excellent, inexpensive food court. It rivals the Grand Indonesia mall nearby for top-end cred. (www. plazaindonesia.com; Jl Thamrin 28-30; ⏱10am-10pm; 🛜)

Grand Indonesia

MALL

40 🏠 MAP P80, B4

This luxury mall contains a plethora of high-end fashion outlets, plus high-street favourites like Uniqlo and Zara. There is also a number of good local and international restaurants, and a multiscreen cinema (p92). It sprawls over eight marble-clad floors. (www.grand-indonesia.com; Jl Thamrin 1; ⏱10am-10pm)

Pasar Jl Surabaya

MARKET

41 🏠 MAP P80, G5

Jakarta's most famous street market is in Menteng. It has woodcarvings, furniture, textiles, jewellery, old vinyl records and many (dubious) antiques, from nautical memorabilia to vintage kitchen items. Bargain like crazy. (Jl Surabaya; ⏱8am-5pm)

Eiger Adventure

SPORTS & OUTDOORS

42 🏠 MAP P80, F2

An Indonesian brand selling good-quality outdoor gear and camping equipment for a fraction of the price of Western brands. There is a number of Eiger outlets in Jakarta, including this stand-alone shop on Jl Cikini Raya. (📞021-3193 6217; https://eigeradventure.com; Jl Cikini Raya 51; ⏱9am-10pm)

Cikini Gold Center

JEWELLERY

43 🏠 MAP P80, H5

An enormous mall of small shops and stalls selling all manner of precious goods and jewellery. Take your time to browse the vendors and compare prices. There's something for every budget and most tastes, although most of it is on the bling side. (📞021-3190 9088; Jl Pengangsaan Timur Raya; ⏱10am-5pm)

Sukarno: Indonesia's 'Brother'

An inspirational orator and charismatic leader, Sukarno (1901–70) is still held in great affection and esteem by many older Indonesians, who often refer to him as Bung Karno – bung meaning 'buddy' or 'brother'.

A flamboyant, complicated and highly intelligent character with a Javanese father and Balinese mother, Sukarno was fluent in several languages. His influences, apart from Islam, included Marxism, Javanese and Balinese mysticism, a mainly Dutch education and the theosophy movement. He had nine wives (with up to four at once) at a time when polygamy was no longer very common in Indonesia.

A year after graduating as a civil engineer and architect in 1926, he was elected the first leader of the pro-independence Indonesian National Party (PNI). Because of his political activities he spent several years during the 1930s either in prison or exiled in the outer reaches of the archipelago.

Dutch colonial rule came to an end with the Japanese occupation in 1942 and the name 'Jakarta' was restored. On 17 August 1945 Sukarno and his deputy Mohammad Hatta declared Indonesia's independence in Jakarta. When the Japanese left at the end of WWII, the Dutch returned and tried to re-establish colonial rule. But it was too late, and after much bloodshed, a peace agreement paved the way for the Indonesian flag to rise over Istana Merdeka on 27 December 1949.

During the 1950s and into the 1960s, Sukarno tried to turn Jakarta into his idea of a modern city. Jalan Thamrin was built, along with the Monas in Merdeka Square and the Hotel Indonesia. This process continued after General Suharto took power in 1965, with new schemes constantly being announced to keep up with the waves of poor immigrants from rural Indonesia.

Following Suharto's coup, Sukarno spent the last five years of his life under house arrest. Throughout his political career he strove to unite Indonesians and, more than anyone else, he was the architect and creator of Indonesia.

Explore ◈

Jalan Jaksa Area

Once Jakarta's backpacker haven, the Jalan Jaksa area is now at mid-gentrification stage. Old hostels and flophouses have been replaced by up-market condos and hotels. Its new diversity is reflected in the variety of eateries, both humble and exalted. But best of all, you're just a short walk from much of the best that Jakarta has to offer.

The Short List

◦ **Jl Kampung Lima Food Stalls (p101)** *Sample local foods as you bounce from one excellent purveyor to another.*

◦ **Sarinah Thamrin Plaza (p107)** *Discover goods and treasures from across Indonesia.*

◦ **Bersih Sehat Menteng (p101)** *Relax and revive at this professionally run spa.*

◦ **Shanghai Blue 1920 (p103)** *Dine like you've time travelled to 1920s Shangha*

◦ **Awan Lounge (p105)** *Sip and adult beverage here – one of several fine venues for an adult beverage in the neighbourhood.*

Getting There & Around

🚗 The area is well served by taxis, Grab and Go-Jek.

🚌 This area, near Jl Thamrin, is good for the Transjakarta bus lines.

🚌 Gambir train station, Jakarta's busiest, is a 10- to 20-minute walk from this neighbourhood.

Neighbourhood Map on p100

Walking Tour 🚶

Savouring Street Life

Amid glitzy towers and mega-developments, you can still experience a charming Jakarta at street level. The area east of Jl Thamrin has pockets of local life and rewards people who stroll.

Start Warung Ngalam
(🚉 Sarinah)

End Kopi Oey Sabang
(🚉 Bank Indonesia)

Length 700m; 30 minutes

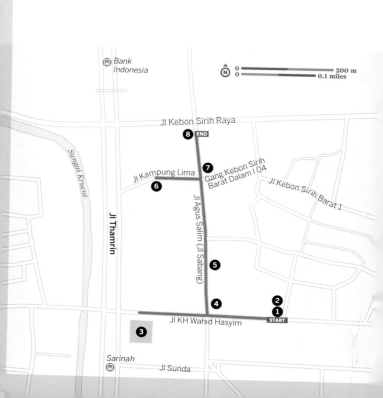

❶ Warung Ngalam

A warung (food stall) for a new age. This open-sided cafe (p101) serves delicious Indonesian dishes with many Asian influences. Patrons adore the crispy duck, fried tofu, fish-head soup, homemade noodles and more. Vegetables are fresh and varied. Expect to wait for a seat around lunch-time.

❷ Bersih Sehat Menteng

The sophisticated massage and sauna facilities (p101) have very professional masseurs. This spa is highly recommended.

❸ Sarinah Thamrin Plaza

Check out Jakarta's original department store (p107), which has an excellent range of regional handicrafts. Best of all, prices are both fixed and fair. Devote your energies to finding your own personal treasure.

❹ Restoran Garuda Sabang

A popular, 24-hour restaurant (though smoky and fluorescent-lit) serving freshly made Padang food that throbs with Bollywood tunes and Indo-pop. Small dishes of tempting flavours – including jackfruit curry, chilli prawns, *tempe penyet* (fried tempeh with spicy sauce), *rendang* (beef coconut curry), and potato and corn fritters – are brought to your table with great speed (p104):

❺ Timeless Shops

North on Jl Agus Salim, the east side of the street still has a row of classic old shops. None is individually notable, but together they evoke an Asia that is rapidly being replaced by rising affluence and development. Here you'll find cheap plastic household goods, oddball toys, books fresh off the photocopier and enormous bags of bargain rice.

❻ Jalan Kampung Lima Food Stalls

In the shadow of the Mandiri Bank headquarters, there is a tiny lane lined with food stalls (p101). Tarps overhead provide shade for tiny stools and tables where you can enjoy fresh-to-the-minute Indonesian fare. There are dozens of stalls serving everything from smoothies to curries to spicy fried chicken. Finish your meal with *piseng goreng* (fried banana).

❼ Sakura Anpan

Satisfy your sweet cravings by sampling the delicious treats on display at this old-school bakery (p101).

❽ Kopi Oey Sabang

This is a wonderful little cafe (p106) that has been modelled on an old Chinese teahouse. It is part of a national chain that serves Vietnamese coffee, turmeric tea and snacks that reflect Indonesia's heritage.

Jalan Jaksa Area

For reviews see

◎ Sights		p101
⊗ Eating		p101
⊗ Drinking		p105
⊖ Shopping		p107

MENTENG

Jl Menteng Raya

Jl Menteng Raya

Jl Prapatan

Tugu
1 Tani

Jl Menteng Raya

Jl Wahid Hasyim IV

Jl Menteng

Jl Menteng Kecil

Gondangdia

Jl Cut Nyak Dien

Jl Cut Nyak Dien

Jl Menteng

Jl Wahid Hasyim

Jl Johar

Jl Kebon Sirih Raya

Jl Kebon Sirih Timur

Gang 1

⊗12

Gang 3

15

Jl Jaksa

⊗14

Gg 3 Timur

Jl Jaksa

13 ⊗

Jl Kebon Sirih Barat 1

Jl Kebon Sirih Barat 2

Jl Cokroaminoto

Jl KH Wahid Hasyim

Jl Sumatera

Jl Sumbawa

Bersih
Sehat
Menteng

2 ◎⊗
3 ⊗

Jl Kebon Sirih Raya

⊗9

⊗5

Jl Kampung Lima

16 ⊖

⊗11
⊗6

Jl Agus Salim (Jl Sabang)

Jl Gereja Theresia

8 ⊗⊗
10

Jl Sunda

Bank
Indonesia

Jakarta Visitor
Information
Office

Jakarta
Theatre

⊗4

⊖18

19 ⊖

Jl Thamrin

Jl Thamrin

Sarinah

17

Jl KH Wahid Hasyim

⊗7

0   200 m
0   0.1 miles

Sights

Tugu Tani   MONUMENT

1 ◎ MAP P100, F1

A post-independence and appealingly bombastic statue depicting a farmer who became a soldier in the fight for independence from the Dutch. It shows the widespread grassroots struggle to shrug off colonialism and take ownership of land and community again. (Farmer's Monument; off Jl Menteng Raya)

Bersih Sehat Menteng   MASSAGE

2 ◎ MAP P100, C3

The hygienic and elegant massage and sauna facilities and professional masseurs at this spa are highly recommended. Find it in the complex behind the small Warung Ngalam restaurant. (☏021-390 0204; www.bersihsehat.com; 1st fl, Jl KH Wahid Hasyim 106; 1hr massage 170,000Rp; ⊙10am-9pm)

Eating

Warung Ngalam   INDONESIAN $

3 ✖ MAP P100, C3

A warung (food stall) for a new age. This narrow, open-sided cafe with single seating serves delicious Indonesian dishes with a panoply of Asian influences. Patrons swoon over crispy duck, fried tofu, fish-head soup, homemade noodles and more.

Vegetables are fresh and varied. Expect to wait for a seat around lunch-time. (☏021-391 2483; Jl KH Wahid Hasyim 106; mains 20,000-45,000Rp; ⊙9am-10pm)

Jl Kampung Lima Food Stalls   INDONESIAN $

4 ✖ MAP P100, A2

Look in the shadow of the Mandiri Bank headquarters and you'll discover this tiny lane lined with food stalls. Tarps overhead provide shade to tiny stools and tables where you can slurp up fresh-to-the-minute Indonesian fare. Choose from dozens of stalls serving everything from smoothies and curries to spicy fried chicken. Finish your meal with *piseng goreng* (fried banana). (Jl Kampung Lima, off Jl Thamrin; mains from 20,000Rp; ⊙8am-10pm)

Sakura Anpan   BAKERY $

5 ✖ MAP P100, B2

Surrounded by old-school shops (Want a photocopied book? Ribbons? Plastic toys?) this retro bakery has long display cases filled with tempting baked goods. Cupcakes, doughnuts, pies, cakes and other sweet goodness all hit the spot. (☏021-314 4253; Jl Agus Salim 25; items from 10,000Rp; ⊙7am-8pm)

Jl KH Wahid Hasyim Food Stalls   INDONESIAN $

6 ✖ MAP P100, B3

Although there are a few stalls cooking up food by day, after dark,

Seeking a Sustainable Future: Jakarta Today

The official population of Jakarta is around 10 million, but the figure is far from exact. The city's economic magnetism draws in countless more from across the nation daily. This huge mass of people means that Jakarta is a frenetic place that always seems close to complete chaos. Trying to bring order to the city and give it a sustainable future is the number-one topic – and challenge.

When much-loved local governor Joko Widodo was elected president in 2014, his successor was Basuki Tjahaja Purnama, universally called Ahok. Being both Christian and Chinese, Ahok was not the obvious leader for the capital of the world's largest Muslim nation. However, by catering to the enormous needs of the poor, instituting plans to clean up the city, and taking on corruption in an effective manner Ahok won over scores of sceptics.

However, it was an issue of alleged blasphemy that proved Ahok's downfall. A speech he had given contained an offhand reference to a Quran verse and this soon led to protests. In November 2016, more than 100,000 people – many brought in from conservative areas of Java well outside Jakarta – marched, rallied and rioted in central Jakarta amid calls for Ahok to resign and be put on religious trial.

As a result, a new Jakarta governor, Anies Baswedan, took office in 2017; he was previously a student activist and the Minister of Education and Culture. He made various attempts to clean up the city before the Asian Games in 2018, including putting a giant nylon net over polluted and foul-smelling rivers to minimise the stench and visible debris on the surface after supposed initial river clean-up attempts weren't enough.

During his governorship, Jakarta police shot dozens of alleged petty criminals in the lead-up to the games, and arrested hundreds. This hard-line approach was believed to deter others from committing crimes during the games. After considering the Asian Games a great success, the city was on a high, and the authorities have put in a bid for the 2032 Olympics.

the uneven streets here morph into more of a cluster. Don't expect dozens of choices, but you will find several frequent vendors cooking up nasi goreng and other late-night staples of the Jakarta diet. (cnr Jl KH Wahid Hasyim & Jl Agus Salim; mains from 15,000Rp; ⊙10am-late)

Waha Kitchen ASIAN $$

7 ⊗ MAP P100, A3

A fittingly fashionable bistro occupies the lobby of the designer Kosenda Hotel with a 24-hour bar and a menu of modern Asian dishes. Food appears to be served with a Western palate in mind, with classic but well-executed dishes like spicy seafood noodles, Hainanese chicken rice, black pepper beef, and roasted duck and pineapple curry. Cocktails and mocktails too. Plus, fresh juices, beers and imported wines. (☎021-3193 6868; www.waha kitchen.com; Kosenda Hotel, Jl KH Wahid Hasyim 127; mains 78,000-158,000Rp; ⊙24hr)

Honu Poke & Matcha Bar HAWAIIAN $$

8 ⊗ MAP P100, B4

Jakarta has joined the poke revolution. This cool little local chain serves 10 varieties of the Hawaiian protein bowls. The 'torched' bowl comes with flame-seared salmon, salmon belly, shiitake, red radish, edamame, nori and *tobiko* (flying-fish roe). There's also raw tuna, tofu and

chicken options, all served with veggies on a bed of rice. Wash it down with matcha, a cold brew or fresh juice. There's also a branch in South Jakarta (☎021-7179 3580; Jl Kemang Selatan 125). (☎021-2123 1449; Jl Agus Salim 60; poke bowls 50,000-90,000Rp; ⊙10am-9.30pm Tue-Sun)

Shanghai Blue 1920 CHINESE, INDONESIAN $$

9 ⊗ MAP P100, B2

Dine like you've time travelled to 1920s Shanghai in an atmospheric room loaded with tapestries, wood carvings, red lanterns and flamboyant furnishings (some rescued from an old Batavia tea-house). Standouts from the menu include crab-stuffed lychee, fried Shanghai street dumplings, and roasted duck marinated in 12 spices and served with hoi-sin sauce. (☎021-391 8690; www.tuguhotels.com; Jl Kebon Sirih Raya 77-79; dishes 58,000-108,000Rp; ⊙11am-11pm)

Roca Restaurant INTERNATIONAL $$

10 ⊗ MAP P100, B4

Inside Artotel Thamrin (p104) Roca serves mostly Western dishes all day every day in a fun space with art on the ceiling and a choice of communal tables or lounge chairs. Dishes range from solid brunch options like eggs Florentine to chicken tostada salad, sharing tapas platters (with cheese, aioli and chicken

Artotel Thamrin

Worth a look, even if you're not staying the night, is the hip hotel **Artotel Thamrin** (see **10** Map p100, B4; ☑021-3192 5888; www.artotelindonesia.com; Jl Sunda 3; r incl breakfast from 805,000Rp; 🅿❄🛜),You can't miss the building as it's covered in an enormous pink, white and black illustration. Eight Indonesian artists were each given one floor to decorate and told to go wild. The results are stunning and striking. Motifs range from cartoonish to graffiti to minimalist chic. No matter the style, furnishings are luxe and there are oodles of amenities.

skewers), pizza, burgers, pasta, steak and roast chicken. (www.artotelindonesia.com/thamrin-jakarta; Jl Sunda 3; breakfast from 63,000Rp, mains 79,000-188,000Rp; 🕲24hr)

Restoran Garuda Sabang   INDONESIAN $$

11 🍴 MAP P100, B3

A smoky, no-frills, fluorescent-lit, all-day, all-night depot of locally loved Padang food goodness, it's sometimes throbbing with Bollywood tunes or Indo-pop and often packed with locals. Little flavourful dishes are piled on your table at lightning speed: jackfruit curry, chilli prawns, *tempe penyet*

(fried tempeh with spicy sauce), *rendang* (beef coconut curry), and potato and corn fritters. It's all made fresh. (☑021-314 2466; www.restorangaruda.com; Jl Agus Salim 59; mains from 35,000Rp; 🕲24hr; 🛜)

Sate Khas Senayan   INDONESIAN $$

12 🍴 MAP P100, D1

An air-conditioned Indonesian chain restaurant known for its decent *sate* (skewers of chicken, beef and lamb), plus Indonesian favourites like *ayam goreng kremes* (fried chicken in batter), *gurame bakar* (grilled fish) and *nasi campur* (rice with a choice of side dishes). Look out for regional specialities, and wash them down with a durian juice or Bintang. Indonesian breakfast options also available.

It's on Jl Kebon Sirih Raya at the northern end of Jl Jaksa. (☑021-3192 6238; www.sarirasa.co.id; Jl Kebon Sirih Raya 31A; breakfast from 18,000Rp, mains 30,000-110,000Rp; 🕲8am-11pm Sun-Thu, to midnight Fri & Sat; ❄🛜)

Ocha & Bella   ITALIAN $$$

13 🍴 MAP P100, D3

You could travel around the world to Milan, or you can have a stylish Italian experience right here. Choose a table in the minimalist glass-fronted dining room or take the breeze on the terrace. Italian classics include risotto, pasta and pizza (cooked in a clay oven).

Meanwhile, there's Wagyu striploin and a range of Asian mains to provide contrast. (021-310 5999; Morrissey Hotel, Jl KH Wahid Hasyim 70; mains 80,000-600,000Rp; 11am-midnight Sun-Thu, to 1am Fri & Sat)

Ya Udah Bistro — GERMAN $$

14 ☒ MAP P100, D3

Jakarta's most culturally inappropriate restaurant serves all manner of pork dishes, which you can wash down with copious amounts of German beer. The lacklustre interior with orange and green walls is open to the street and remains shadowy even by day. Choose from sausages, pork and beef steaks plus a smattering of sandwiches, burgers and pastas. Smoking is allowed.

American breakfasts come with real bacon. (021-314 0343; www.yaudahbistro.com; Jl Johar 15; mains 49,000-92,000Rp; 8am-midnight Sun-Thu, to 2am Fri & Sat;)

Drinking

Awan Lounge — BAR

Set on the top floor of Kosenda Hotel (see 7 ☒ Map p100, A3), this lovely rooftop garden bar manages to be both understated and dramatic. There's a vertical garden, ample tree cover, plenty of private nooks flickering with candlelight, and a vertigo-inducing glass skylight that plummets nine floors down.

It has a tasty bar menu, electronica thumps at a perfect

Ayam goreng kremes

Indonesian Respite

Think of the Jakartan neighbourhood as your Indonesian respite. Everything you could want – from restful accommodation and excellent non-flashy food to vendors and shops selling anything you might need – can be found close by along mostly tree-shaded streets.

volume and the crowd is mixed local and expat. Weekends can get overly crowded. (☑021-3193 6868; www.awanlounge.com; Jl KH Wahid Hasyim 127; mixed drinks & cocktails/ beers from 80,000/45,000Rp; ☺5pm-1am Sun-Thu, to 2am Fri & Sat)

Coffee Theory

CAFE

15 MAP P100, D2

Find this welcoming little coffee shop next to a huge, bright street-art piece, around the corner from **Hostel 35** (☑021-392 0331; Jl Kebon Sirih Barat I 76). All beans here are sourced from Java and can be prepared using manual methods (V60, Vietnam drip etc). It also serves up teas and smoothies. (☑0878 818 9432; https://thecoffeetheory-chapterjaksa. business.site; Jl Jaksa 4; coffee from 20,000Rp; ☺11am-9pm Mon-Thu, 1-11pm Fri, 2pm-midnight Sat & Sun)

Kopi Oey Sabang

CAFE

16 MAP P100, B2

This gorgeous little cafe, modelled on an old Chinese teahouse, is part of a national chain – there's another branch in Kota (☑021-2937 9290; Green Central City, Jl Gajah Mada 188; menu items & coffee from 20,000Rp; ☺9am-midnight). It comes with antique tiles and vintage prints on the walls, marble tabletops, birdcage lanterns and a great selection of drinks, including Vietnamese coffee and turmeric tea, as well as snacks that reflect Indonesia's heritage, and French toast and Padang-style *roti*. (☑021-3193 4438; www.kopioey.com; Jl Agus Salim 16A; coffee from 25,000Rp; ☺9am-11pm; 🛜)

Jaya Pub

PUB

17 MAP P100, A3

In a dimly lit car park off the main street, this place has a clandestine feel – but it's more on the sleazy than hipster speakeasy side. Still, it's a much beloved pub attracting an older crowd. The bluesy, rock and jazz cover bands are always upbeat. The dance floor gets going after 10pm. Also serves bar snacks, sandwiches and simple mains. (☑021-3192 5633; Jl Thamrin 12; ☺5pm-1am Sun-Thu, to 2am Fri & Sat)

Sarinah Thamrin Plaza

Djakarta Cafe LOUNGE

18 📞 MAP P100, B3

One of the few spots in the area to grab a cold beer after hours is this worn 24-hour diner decked out in retro 1930s decor. Enjoy a drink on its outdoor terrace or inside where there's air-conditioning. Unspectacular dishes include Indonesian and Western mains (like fried rice, chicken quesadilla, and fish and chips). It has a few dozen wine choices. (📞021-316 0316; Jl Thamrin 9; mains 55,000-300,000Rp, wine from 120,000Rp; ⏰24hr; 🛜)

Shopping

Sarinah Thamrin Plaza DEPARTMENT STORE

19 🔒 MAP P100, A3

Jakarta's original department store is known for its handicrafts, which are sourced from across the archipelago. The batik selection is excellent. (📞021-3192 3008; www.sarinah.co.id; Jl Thamrin 11; ⏰10am-10pm)

Worth a Trip 👓
Taman Mini Indonesia Indah

TMII, the 'Beautiful Indonesia Miniature Park',
covers over 1 sq km and has full-scale traditional
houses for each of Indonesia's provinces, with
displays of regional handicrafts and clothing, and
even a mini-scale Borobudur temple. Museums,
theatres and an IMAX cinema are scattered
throughout the grounds. With amusement parks
for kids and a small water park, you can easily
spend an entire day here.

Beautiful Indonesia
Miniature Park; TMII
📞021-8779 2078
www.tamanmini.com
Jl Raya Taman Mini
15,000Rp
🕐7am-10pm; 👫

Mini Indonesia

TMII has kept up with Indonesia's changing geography since it opened in 1975. Where there were originally 27 full-scale traditional houses from Indonesia's 27 provinces, there are now 33. Also, after East Timor seceded in 2002, its display was converted to the Museum of East Timor. Each of the houses has displays of regional handicrafts and clothing. All are built around a large 'lagoon' where you can row around the major islands of the archipelago. Putting the 'mini' in the name is the pint-sized version of the Borobudur Temple.

Rides

There are no thrill rides, but you can get around the park on bike, on a mini-train, in a swan paddleboat or by cable car.

Museums

Within the park, and just outside it, there are plenty of museums. Two of the more interesting ones are the Museum Asmat, containing an excellent collection of woodcarvings from the famed Irian Jaya tribe, and the Museum Indonesia, the most important museum in the park with costumes and ethnographic exhibits from all over the country.

The Soldier's Museum (Museum Prep-rajuritan) is a Camelot-style building featuring warriors from around Indonesia, while the Museum Fauna features an enclosure with fearsome Komodo dragons.

Amusements

Kids love the Istana Anak-Anak Indonesia (Castle of Indonesian Children), which is quite elaborate and, we have to say, closely resembles the centrepiece castle you'd find at a Disney park. For digital thrills, there's an IMAX theatre.

★ Top Tips

o Virtually every attraction, activity, museum and more carries a separate fee (from 2000Rp to 75,000Rp), which means that the costs for a visit can rapidly add up.

o Free cultural performances are staged in selected regional houses (usually around 10am); Sunday is the big day for cultural events, but shows are also held during the week.

✕ Take a Break

Bebek Renon is a Balinese restaurant in the park that specialises in duck. Try the fried version, which is marinated in fragrant spices, then cooked until it is perfectly tender.

★ Getting There

🚍 The park is 18km southwest of Jakarta's centre.

🚕 A taxi takes 45 to 90 minutes and costs up to 150,000Rp.

Explore ✦

South Jakarta

Jakarta's sprawling south has vast kampung (the traditional villages where most Jakartans live) punctuated by islands and ribbons of glitz, wealth and bohemian hang-outs. Malls as flashy as any in the world and posh hotels anchor huge office developments. Amid this are neighbourhoods with real personalities, like captivating Kemang with its array of restaurants, ubercool coffee houses and trendy boutiques. After dark, some of Jakarta's legendary clubs still party the night away.

The Short List

○ **Jakarta War Cemetery (p112)** *Stroll through this serene resting place for casualties deceased from WWII.*

○ **Museum Layang-Layang (p118)** *Explore this storehouse of kites in all shapes and sizes.*

○ **Aksara (p130)** *Browse this fine bookshop with a cafe and creative classes.*

○ **Dragonfly (p126)** *Dress up for a night out at this legendary dance club.*

○ **Pasar Santa (p130)** *Peruse this mall's 2nd floor, which offers dozens of creative booths run by hipster entrepreneurs.*

Getting There & Around

🚃 Blok M is a major stop for several Transjakarta lines that run along the major thoroughfares.

🚕 Taxis and other rides such as *ojeks* (motorcycle taxis) and Grab are the main ways most people get around in the south. Do take account of rush hour traffic though when planning journeys.

Neighbourhood Map on p116

South Jakarta skyline CREATIVA IMAGES/SHUTTERSTOCK ©

Top Sight 📷
Jakarta War Cemetery

Thousands of people, including those from Dutch and British Commonwealth armed forces, were killed by the Japanese in and around Jakarta during WWII. This cemetery was established after the war to bring together the military and civilian deceased from across Indonesia. It's a beautiful and serene place in the midst of Jakarta.

◉ MAP P116, E2

www.ogs.nl

Jl Menteng Pulo Raya

free

🕗 8am-5pm

The Dutch

The larger part of the cemetery is managed by the Dutch, who built a beautiful memorial building, complete with a chapel and a dignified bell tower. An adjoining open-air courtyard contains more than 700 urns holding the remains of Dutch people who died in Japanese POW camps. However, out amid more than 4300 rigidly ordered grave markers (pictured), you'll see many with dates of death after WWII (specifically 1945 to 1949). Here lie the Dutch soldiers who were killed trying to keep Indonesia under colonial rule. What's sadly missing is any mention of the tens of thousands of Indonesian military and civilians who died during the conflict.

The Commonwealth

Administered by the UK, the Commonwealth portion of the cemetery opened in 1961. Tellingly, the original plans have the notation with an arrow that reads 'Jakarta approx. 7 miles'. One look at the high-rise apartment blocks, hotels and office buildings looming on all sides today is a testament to Jakarta's sprawl.

Throughout the cemetery you'll discover myriad stories. There are names of people who came from countries the world over and who never returned home. In the British section, a series of headstones is devoted to those who died because of the sinking of the *Empress of Asia,* a passenger liner that was sunk bringing Allied troops to Singapore in 1942. Many of the crew were taken prisoner and later died. Today you can get snippets of their stories from tombstones that bear their titles, such as 'bartender'.

Other Cemeteries

Some of Jakarta's largest cemeteries are just north of the war cemetery. You'll find sections for Chinese, Muslims and many more ethnicities and faiths.

★ Top Tips

○ If the entrance gates are locked on weekdays, look through the iron grills and wave to the gardeners who will be happy to let you in.

○ Bring your phone. Many of the memorials give scant details of the events that led to the deaths of the people interred. But with a little online searching, you can uncover often-compelling details.

✖ Take a Break

A 10-minute walk south will take you to the dozens of restaurants and vendors at the luxe Kota Kasablanka (p133) mall, which also has a Carrefour supermarket.

The fancy Henshin (p124) sky restaurant at the Westin hotel is a short trip away by car.

Walking Tour 🥾

Browsing Kemang

Don't miss the more-easily walkable streets in Kemang, the most stylish place in Jakarta to stroll outside of a mall. The ever-changing and creative assortment of galleries, shops, cafes, restaurants and lounges make a walk here feel a bit like a treasure hunt. You can easily spend the better part of a day making discoveries and enjoying indulgences.

Walk Facts

Start dia.lo.gue artspace (Jl Kemang Selatan 99)

End Colony mall (Jl Kemang Raya)

Length 2km; one hour

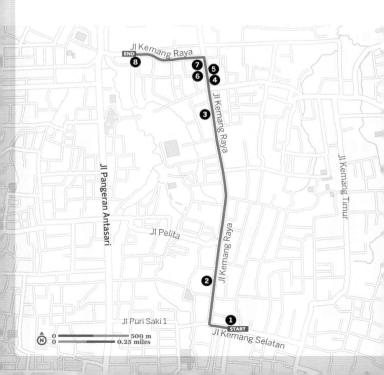

❶ dia.lo.gue artspace

Contemporary art exhibitions, along with stylish designer goods, books and good coffee are availablein this modish space (p130). There's also a cafe on-site, serving breakfast, pasta, Asian plates and other mains.

❷ LoCarasa

This fashionable cafe (p119) has several handmade pizza varieties (or craft your own). You can also make a variety of pasta bowls.

❸ Queen's Head

This popular lounge/pub (p122) combines Balinese style with a geometric design and modern versions of British pub fare. There's an outdoor area and top cocktails are available at the bar well into the early hours.

❹ One Fifteenth Coffee

This Indonesian Barista Championship–winning small chain (p126) is famed for its exceptional coffee. The Kemang Raya branch is no exception, with flavoursome coffee and perfectly executed food.

❺ Qonita Batik

This design store (p133) sells its own line of Javanese batik clothing that is popular with locals.

❻ Aksara

This hip hang-out (p130) has a wide selection of books (many in English) along with fine stationery and writing accessories, and is a must-stop for anyone interested in words on paper. There's also a small cafe serving coffee and cakes.

❼ Relax Living

This full-service spa (p129) offers a full range of therapies and treatments in an calm and perfumed atmosphere.

❽ Colony

This unassuming mall (p133) has a great selection of interesting shops, cafes and restaurants to check out.

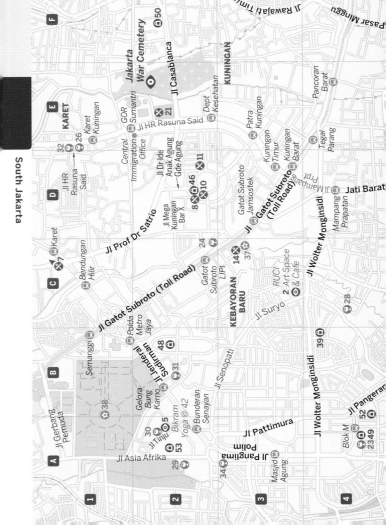

South Jakarta

5

6

7

8

Jl Raya

F

Jl Kemang Raya

🔵 25

🔵 12

Relax
Living

🔵 15

🔴 17

🔴 40

🔴 36

Cat 4
Cabin

Jl Kemang Raya

🔴 18 ✕ 16

🔴 13 ✕

🔴 43 🔴

✕ 54

E

🔵 45

0   400 m

0   0.2 miles

Jl Kemang Raya

Duren
Tiga

🔴 Jati Barat

Jati Barat

🔵 Imigrasi

KEMANG

Jl Kemang Timur

🔴 Gudang-Gudang

Jl Kemang Yoga Studio

Warung
Jati

🔴 27

🔴 3

See Enlargement

Jl Kemang Raya

🔴 20

🔴 9

🔴 6 ✕

✕ 22

Jl Kemang Selatan

🔴 41

Jl Pejaten Barat Raya

Jl Ampera Raya

🔴 35

🔴 19 ✕

🔴 51

Jl Taman
Kemang

Jl Kemang Raya

Jl Pangeran Antasari

🔴 42

🔴 33

Jamu
Body
Treatment

Jl Cipete Raya

🔴 47

🔴 44

Jl Panglima Polim

Jl Panglima Polim

Jl Pangeran Antasari

Jl Panglima Polim

Antasari

For reviews see

🔵	Top Sights	p112
🔵	Sights	p118
✕	Eating	p119
🔵	Drinking	p125
🔴	Entertainment	p129
🔴	Shopping	p130

0   1 km

0   0.5 miles

N

Sights

Museum Layang-Layang

MUSEUM

1 👁 MAP P116, A8

Families will love Jakarta's kite museum, located in a quiet backstreet in Pondok Labu, South Jakarta. Inside a traditional Indonesian house, complete with courtyard, there's a collection of around 600 kites. A 10-minute educational video explains the different styles and origins of kite flying (and that it probably all started in Indonesia). The impressive range of kites includes a giant horse and cart, dragon, ship and lion fish, plus flat kites made of bamboo and banana-tree leaves. As part of the entrance fee, visitors can make and decorate their own kite to take home. (Kites Museum of Indonesia; 📞021-765 8075; Jl H Kamang 38; 15,000Rp; ⏱9am-4pm; 👪)

RUCI Art Space & Cafe

GALLERY

2 👁 MAP P116, C3

RUCI Art Space has become a favourite on the city's burgeoning art scene. Occupying an industrial space in the hip neighbourhood of Senopati, the gallery hosts regular solo and group exhibitions from local contemporary artists. Work ranges from painting and photography to installation art. A large cafe is attached, decorated with designer furniture and selling drinks (coffee from 30,000Rp), mains (noodle and rice dishes from 55,000Rp and tacos from 35,000Rp) and desserts (milk fritters, panna cotta, and cinnamon banana fritters from 35,000Rp). (📞021-7279 9769; http://ruciart.com; Jl Suryo Blok S 49; ⏱gallery 11am-7pm, cafe 10am-midnight Mon-Thu, to 1am Fri & Sat)

Gudang-Gudang Yoga Studio

YOGA

3 👁 MAP P116, C8

Get away from the urban hustle and bustle at this one-of-a-kind yoga studio and sanctuary of peace. Experienced yogis and beginners are welcome at a range of classes that include vinyasa, Jivamukti and other meditations. Classes in the traditional Javanese *joglo* hut are particularly atmospheric – with the soothing sounds of a water fountain. There's a cafe next door. (📞021-718 0173; www.gudanggudangyoga.com; Jl Kemang Timur 88; drop-in classes 110,000Rp; ⏱8am-4pm)

Cat Cabin

WILDLIFE WATCHING

4 👁 MAP P116, E5

Feline fans can hang out with the 15 well-groomed and looked-after cats at this living-room-style cafe. You're welcome to stroke and make a fuss of the hairy creatures (some are pedigree) and take as many photos as you like – the star is the cute cat who likes wearing a bow tie. Drinks and mains can also be ordered. (📞021-7179 5243; www.thecatcabinjakarta.com; Jl Kemang Raya 31; entry per hour Mon-Fri 60,000Rp, Sat & Sun 65,000Rp; ⏱9am-9pm Tue-Thu, 10am-10pm Fri & Sun)

Bikram Yoga @ 42

5 MAP P116, A2

Runs around 10 yoga classes per day, from Bikram to hot barre, Ashtanga and anti-gravity yoga. The studio has a small cafe and sportswear shop attached. (📞021-5790 1261; http://bikramyogajakarta.com; level 2, Plaza Senayan Arcadia; drop-in classes 195,000Rp, weekly unlimited pass 695,000Rp; ⏱class times vary)

Eating

Mie Chino Pasar Santa

INDONESIAN $

The hipster haven of Pasar Santa (see **39** 🍴 Map p116, B4) has a charming little independent market on the top floor. Here, stalls sell food that stems from the culinary dreams of young chefs. This no-frills budget joint has only three things on the menu – meatballs, dumplings and unbelievably tasty bowls of chicken and mushroom noodles. Believe us, they must be tried. (Pasar Santa, Jl Cipaku I; mains from 18,000Rp; ⏱noon-9pm Tue-Sun)

LoCarasa

PIZZA $

6 ❌ MAP P116, C7

Inside this industrial-chic cafe choose from several handmade super-thin-crust (or thick-crust if you prefer) pizza varieties, or craft your own. You can also make a variety of pasta bowls, from cheesy fettuccine to sliced beef with BBQ sauce fusilli. Sweet treats include Nutella cake and pancakes, plus cannoli stuffed with cream. Savour it all on the

Museum Layang-Layang

Jakarta's Contemporary Art Scene

The galleries in the wealthier neighbourhoods of Jakarta, such as Kemang, are the epicentre of Indonesia's contemporary art scene, which has flourished in recent years with a panoply of installations, sculptures, performance art and more. It can be extremely original, eye-catching and thought-provoking – or the opposite.

Opened in late 2017, **Museum Macan** (Museum of Modern & Contemporary Art in Nusantara; ☏021-2212 1888; www.museummacan. org; Jl Panjang Raya 5, Kebon Jeruk; exhibitions 50,000-100,000Rp; ⏰10am-7pm Tue-Sun) is Indonesia's first modern and contemporary art museum and an exciting cultural development for the city. It was built to house the private art collection of businessman Haryanto Adikoesoemo, who has amassed some 800 works by Indonesian artists.

Past exhibitions include a travelling survey of Yayoi Kusama and major show of Asian artists: Arahmaiani, Lee Mingwei and On Kawara

Every two years there's also the **Jakarta Biennale** (http://jakartabiennale.net), which is held in Gudang Sarinah Ekosistem and several other Jakarta public institutions.

Traditionally, painting was an art for decorating palaces and places of worship, typically with religious or legendary subject matter. Foreign artists in Bali in the 1930s inspired a revolution in painting: artists began to depict everyday scenes on new, more realistic, less crowded canvases. Others developed an attractive 'primitivist' style.

Much local art today is mass-produced tourist-market stuff, though there are also talented and original artists. Indonesia's most celebrated 20th-century painter was the Javanese expressionist Affandi (1907–90), who liked to paint by squeezing the paint straight out of the tube.

To find out about the latest exhibitions and art shows, search coverage in the online news site **Jakarta Globe** (www.thejakartaglobe.com) and the cultural content of the printed **Jakarta Post** (www.thejakartapost.com).

shaded terrace. (☎021-719 1808; Jl Kemang Raya 88; mains from 28,000Rp; ⊙8am-1am Sun-Thu, to 2.30am Fri & Sat)

Blue Terrace
HEALTH FOOD $$

7 ❌ MAP P116, C1

Counteract some of Jakarta's toxins at Blue Terrace, which crafts beautifully presented dishes for the health conscious. The menu is chock-full of colourful salads and mains, all delicately arranged and many garnished with edible flowers. The seared yellow fin tuna with quinoa, beetroot, capsicum, roasted cherry tomato, quail egg and pesto dressing is simply divine. (☎021-251 0888; www.ayana.com; Ayana Midplaza Hotel, Jl Jenderal Sudirman Kav 10-11; mains from 65,000Rp; ⊙7am-9pm)

Din Tai Fung
CHINESE $$

This branch of the Michelin-starred Taiwanese dumpling restaurant attached to Bikram Yoga @ 42 pa(see 5 ⊙ Map p116, A2), one of many in Jakarta, is well hidden and has a relaxing ambience. It specialises in *xiaolongbao* (steamed dumplings), and other exceptionally executed dishes. Order delicious *jiaozi* fried dumplings, plus crispy fried chicken with chilli, and black pepper tenderloin beef with garlicky green beans.

Note: this culturally appropriate branch has swapped out the pork in its dishes for chicken. (☎021-5790 1288; www.dintaifung.co.id; Plaza Senayan Arcadia, Jl New Delhi 9; 4/6/10 dumplings from 42,000/58,000/90,000Rp;

⊙10.30am-10pm Mon-Thu, 10.30am-11pm Fri, 10am-11pm Sat, 10am-10pm Sun; ✴️🛜)

Loewy
FRENCH $$

8 ❌ MAP P116, D2

One of Jakarta's most popular dining spots, this casual 1940s Paris-meets-New York bistro is located right in the middle of the busiest business district. It serves classic French brasserie (French onion soup or steak frites) and Asian fare (Indonesian short ribs and Hainan chicken). However, it's after dark when Loewy really comes alive – it's staffed by top mixologists. (☎021-2554 2378; http://loewyjakarta.com; Jl Lingkar; mains 85,000-250,000Rp; ⊙7.30am-1am Mon-Fri, 9am-1am Sat & Sun)

Honu Poke
HAWAIIAN $$

9 ❌ MAP P116, C7

Find this hip little poke joint next to the dia.lo.gue artspace (p130). It serves 10 varieties of the popular Hawaiian-style rice bowls heaped with a choice of salmon, tuna, tofu or chicken, plus loads of veggies. Enjoy it with a cup of matcha in a sleek minimalist space. (☎021-7179 3580; Jl Kemang Selatan 125; poke bowls 50,000-90,000Rp; ⊙10am-9.30pm Tue-Sun)

J Sparrow's Bar & Grill
SEAFOOD $$

10 ❌ MAP P116, D2

A nautical art-deco interior, bespoke cocktails and an excellent seafood

Avoid Rush Hour

It sounds obvious but it bears repeating: avoid rush hour! Jakarta's jam-packed roads become utterly coagulated during the morning and evening rush. Spending 90 minutes to travel 4km is not unheard of and the lack of sensible walkways, pedestrian bridges and so on mean that you can't just dive out of your taxi and hoof it. Note that the Transjakarta also gets jammed and several buses may pass you before you can squeeze on.

menu make J Sparrow's one of the most stylish places in Jakarta to grab dinner and drinks. Expect fresh sea produce, including lobster and Cajun prawns, plus meat dishes such as lamb chops and tri-tip beef. Vintage cocktails include New York sours and gin fizzes. (☏021-5010 1819; www.jsparrows.com; Noble House Bldg, 2 Jl Dr Ide Anak Agung Gde Agung; ☺10am-1am Sun-Thu, 11am-2am Fri & Sat)

Atico by Javanegra   SPANISH $$

11   MAP P116, D2

Hip Atico has warehouse-style exposed cables, pipes on the ceiling and hardwood floors. There's a relaxing outside terrace with skyscraper views from which to enjoy a glass of wine. It serves Spanish-Mediterranean fare with a focus on quality ingredients. Order classic small tapas plates such as *patatas bravas* (potatoes in a spicy tomato sauce) or heartier meat dishes. (☏021-2295 8194; www.javanegra gourmet.com; Jl Dr Ide Anak Agung Gde Agung; tapas/meat dishes from 35,000/100,000Rp; ☺7am-1am; ❄)

Mamma Rosy   ITALIAN $$

12   MAP P116, F8

Mamma Rosy is often in the kitchen at this very authentic (and popular) Italian trattoria. With her son Daniel, Mamma has brought a taste of the old world to this bright yellow spot in trendy Kemang. Fresh pasta, pizzas and heartier mains make up the menu. Enjoy the chef's special pesto inside or out in the large walled garden.

It's also one of the few places in Jakarta at which to enjoy a craft beer. Choose from a selection of Henderson Valley bottles (pale ale, amber ale, porters and more). (☏021-7179 1592; www.mammarosy.com; Jl Kemang Raya 58; mains 85,000-280,000Rp; ☺10am-10pm Sun-Thu, to midnight Fri & Sat)

Queen's Head   BRITISH $$

13   MAP P116, F7

Seminyak meets Islington in this popular lounge-pub that combines Balinese style with hip geometric design and a modern take on British pub fare. Fish and chips, roasted pork belly, seafood red curry, beef pie and freshly baked bread are some of the options. There's an outdoor area and the bar serves top cocktails well into the early hours. (☎021-719 6160; www.queens headjakarta.com; Jl Kemang Raya 18C; mains 85,000-235,000Rp; ⊙11.30am-1am Sun-Tue, to 2am Wed-Sat)

Lalla

CAFE $$

14 ⊗ MAP P116, C3

With a ceiling covered in hanging ropes, two bonsai trees in the middle of the dining area and various toys and trinkets attached to the wall, Lalla is not your average cafe setting. This funky eatery serves Latin dishes like ceviche and lamb tacos, plus Asian-inspired rice and grain bowls, and Jakarta-American classics: truffle fries, Wagyu burgers and nachos. (☎021-2793 3287; Four Seasons Hotel, Capital Pl, Jl Jendral Gatot Subroto Kav 18, Kuningan Barat; mains from 90,000Rp; ⊙11.30am-10pm; P 🤶)

Poach'd Brunch & Coffee House

BREAKFAST $$

15 ⊗ MAP P116, F6

In a large space with high windows, exposed brick walls and wooden tables, Poach'd serves its namesake eggs in a variety of ways with all the trimmings, plus specials like Texan brisket, Spanish omelette and Indonesian sambal. Lighter bites include fruit platters and muesli bowls. A handful of lunch options too – steak, lamb, chicken and salmon plates – plus fresh cakes. (☎021-719 0706; https:// poachd-brunch-coffee-house.business. site; Jl Kemang Raya 11; mains 65,000-127,000Rp; ⊙7am-7pm; 🤶)

Brown Bag

SANDWICHES $$

16 ⊗ MAP P116, F6

Sandwich joint serving fresh, handmade combinations – roast chicken and focaccia, tuna and Swiss cheese, BLT, Aussie beef steak in a sub roll and more. It also sells manual and cold brew coffees and does a decent brekkie (eggs Benedict, avo sandwich, waffles, French toast). (☎021-718 1010; http://brownbag.co.id; level 2, Plaza Adorama, Jl Kemang Raya 17; sandwiches/mains 64,000/65,000Rp; ⊙9am-9pm; 🤶)

FJ on 7

INTERNATIONAL $$

Hidden at the top of a tall shopping mall (see 51 🔒 Map p116, B6) is this 7th-floor rooftop haven, with comfy sofas, wicker lampshades, green foliage and terrace views. Dining choices include a smattering of casual Asian and Western dishes including pizza, Mexican rice and Hainan chicken. Drinks range from smoked-apple martinis to candyfloss cosmopolitans. There's often a DJ on the weekends. (☎021-2952 9912; 7th fl, Jl Kemang Raya 6, Colony; mains 90,000-105,000Rp; ⊙11am-midnight Sun-Thu, to 2am Fri & Sat; 🤶)

Ecology Bistro

INTERNATIONAL $$

17 ⊗ MAP P116, E5

Occupying a minimalist space covered in plants (on the outside, natural tones on the inside), this is a cool spot for brunch, lunch or dinner. Dishes include salads,

Gama Tower

Jakarta's boxy and super-modern Gama Tower is currently the city's tallest building, at 310m. It's home to the **Westin** (see 21 Map p116, E2; ☎ 021-2788 7788; www.westinjakarta.com; Jl HR Rasuna Said) hotel and Henshin restaurant with its 360-degree views across the city.

chicken quesadillas, spicy Korean chicken wings, pastas and rice mains. The wooden tables surround a large stage area where regular live bands play jazz and other music. There's also a small bar. (☎ 021-719 1032; http://ecology jkt.com; Jl Kemang Raya 6; dishes 55,000-120,000Rp; ⏰11am-midnight Mon-Fri, to 2am Sat & Sun)

Warung Turki   TURKISH $$

18 ✖ MAP P116, F6

Up-market Ottoman Turkish fare prepared in an enormous wood-fired clay oven with a floor-to-ceiling chimney. Dishes are served in lantern-lit dining areas spanning three floors. The lamb and chicken are slow roasted, the bread homemade and the sweet baklava is deliciously sinful. Enjoy yours on the glass-ceilinged rooftop patio. (☎ 021-2905 5898; http://turkuazrst; Jl Kemang Raya 18A; mains 50,000-195,000Rp; ⏰11.30am-10pm Sun-Thu, to 11.30pm Fri & Sat)

Parc 19   FUSION $$

19 ✖ MAP P116, B6

The industrial design, complete with a brick-and-wood bar and re-claimed wood seating, outdoes the menu here, which wanders from pizza and Cajun chicken to burgers and Asian favourites like Thai beef salad and Balinese crispy duck. There's a stylish, young vibe and a fine terrace on which to enjoy a classic cocktail. (☎ 021-719 9988; www.parc19.com; Jl Taman Kemang 19; mains 80,000-280,000Rp; ⏰11am-midnight Mon-Fri, 9am-2am Sat & Sun)

Nusa   INDONESIAN $$$

20 ✖ MAP P116, C7

Inside this grand old 1920s colonial house is one of Jakarta's best up-market Indonesian restaurants. The menu changes nightly depending on what the chefs source from the best local markets and suppliers. Expect creative inspiration and nuanced flavours. Note that as the restaurant is halal, no alcohol is served. Food styling is elegant; many tables overlook the back garden. (☎ 021-719 3954; www. nusagastronomy.com; Jl Kemang Raya 81; lunch dishes 75,000-170,000Rp, 8-course set dinner menu 850,000Rp; ⏰11am-3pm & 6-11pm Tue-Sat; P)

Henshin   JAPANESE, PERUVIAN $$$

21 ✖ MAP P116, E2

This modern dining room and bar has a futuristic tunnel entrance and gaudy geometric mirrored ceilings. The stunning patio has magnificent views across the city.

Chef Hajime Kasuga serves curious flavour combinations known as Nikkei – Japanese-Peruvian fusion food. Choose à la carte *arroz con pato* (slow-roasted duck, coriander rice and Japanese pumpkin) or ceviche and sashimi. (📞 021-2788 7768; www.henshin jakarta.com; levels 67-69, Westin Jakarta, Jl HR Rasuna Said; dishes 160,000-430,000Rp, 4-course tasting menus from 1,800,000Rp; ⏱ 6pm-1am Sun-Thu, to 2am Fri & Sat)

Toscana ITALIAN $$$

22 🍴 MAP P116, C7

An elegant Italian place with exposed brick walls and white tablecloths renowned for its pizzas (baked in a wood-fired oven) and homemade pasta. Other menu items include risotto, fish and meat dishes like fried tenderloin with bacon or with tomato and melted mozzarella. There's also a good selection of Tuscan wines. Save room for the desserts and gelato. (📞 021-718 1217; www.toscana jakarta.com; Jl Kemang Raya 120; mains 75,000-450,000Rp; ⏱ 11am-11pm)

Drinking

Filosofi Kopi COFFEE

23 📍 MAP P116, A4

Immortalised by the Indonesian coffee-lover's movie *Filosofi Kopi* (the film itself was shot here), this busy cafe does a range of local coffees prepared using siphon, V-60, Aeropress and Vietnam drip. It's a cool little space with exposed brick and illustrations on the walls and is a good spot

Filosofi Kopi

for a break if you've been shopping at nearby Blok M (p133). (☎ 021-7391 0939; http://filosofikopi.id/store; Jl Melawai 6; coffee from 22,000Rp; ⏰ 11am-11pm Mon-Fri, 7am-11pm Sat & Sun; ☜)

Dragonfly
CLUB

24 🚇 MAP P116, C2

In the most unlikely of locations (the lobby of an office building), you'll find this top stop for visiting DJs to Jakarta. Lights are projected onto Dragonfly's mesmerising tunnel-shaped interior, there's a bar at the club's centre and the DJ booth is at the far end. Dragonfly attracts affluent revellers, plus a few insalubrious types. The dress code is strict. (☎ 021-520 6789; www.ismaya.com/dragonfly; Jl Jendral Gatot Subroto Kav 23, Graha BIP; drinks from 80,000Rp; ⏰ 9pm-4am Wed, Fri & Sat)

One Fifteenth Coffee
COFFEE

25 🚇 MAP P116, F7

Named after the perfect water-to-coffee ratio, this Indonesian Barista Championship–winning small chain is known for its minimalist style and exceptional coffee. Kemang Raya's branch is no exception, with simple grey decor and wooden chairs. The coffee is flavoursome and the food perfectly executed. We love the shakshuka with merguez sausage, goat's cheese, baked eggs and flatbread. (☎ 021-7179 1733; www.1-15coffee.com; Jl Kemang Raya 37; coffee from 26,000Rp, dishes 37,000-180,000Rp; ⏰ 7am-9pm; ☜)

St Ali Jakarta
COFFEE

26 🚇 MAP P116, E1

Getting onboard South Jakarta's burgeoning third-wave coffee scene is acclaimed Melbourne roaster St Ali. As well as Indonesian coffees, it does African single-origin pour-overs prepared at its designated brew bar, and offers tasting flights if you want to sample a few. Enjoy your chosen brew on a communal work bench or stall. (☎ 021-5290 6814; www.stali.com.au/jakarta; Setiabudi Bldg 2, Jl HR Rasuna Said, Lippo Kuningan; coffee/flights from 35,000/130,000Rp; ⏰ 7am-8pm; ☜)

Monolog Coffee Company
COFFEE

Serving ethically sourced arabica coffee from Indonesia, its blend is low in acidity and bold in body. This outlet in the Plaza Senayan (see 53 🅐 Map p116, A2). also serves well-crafted sandwiches, burgers, panini, desserts and super juices in a trendy space with exposed brick and beams, and wooden floors. The mega cakes at the counter are too good to resist. There's a full all-day breakfast menu too. (☎ 021-572 5144; www.monolog-coffee.com; coffee from 30,000Rp; ⏰ 7am-10pm)

Say Something Coffee
COFFEE

27 🚇 MAP P116, D7

A nice little Seattle-style coffee shop, with hexagonal floor tiles, locally roasted coffee and creative drinks like red velvet, taro, matcha lattes and avocado coffee smoothies. Menu items include beef sambal and breakfast bratwurst plates. Look out for the fun portafilter door handles as you enter. (☎021-2271 6113; Jl Kemang Timur 998; ⏰8am-8pm)

Leon

BAR, CLUB

28 ⬤ MAP P116, C4

Modern sophisticated warehouse-style bar and club with high ceilings and windows, plus a very well-stocked bar. In the early evening, before crowds arrive to dance to the DJ, sit at the leather bar chairs or on Chesterfield-style couches and order from the full food menu (dishes 45,000Rp to 380,000Rp) or try the bespoke handcrafted cocktails. (☎021-722 1188; www.leonjakarta.com; Jl Wijaya I 25; cocktails from 160,000Rp; ⏰4pm-midnight Mon, to 1am Tue-Thu, to 2am Fri, 11am-2am Sat, 11am-1am Sun)

Brewerkz

MICROBREWERY

29 ⬤ MAP P116, A2

One of the few places serving craft beer in Jakarta is this Singaporean microbrewery that has a bar in the Crystal Lagoon part of Senayan City mall. It's essentially a sports bar, but brews nine beers on-site including an IPA, golden ale, lager and stout, though it's pricey at 135,000Rp a pint. Otherwise go for a tasting paddle. (☎021-2923 5788; www.brewerkz.com; Senayan City, Jl Asia Afrika 19; small beers from 110,000Rp, 4-beer tasting paddle 120,000Rp; ⏰10am-midnight Sun-Thu, to 2am Fri & Sat; 🛜)

Prohibition

COCKTAIL BAR

30 ⬤ MAP P116, A2

Inspired by 1930s-style Shanghai speakeasies, this decadent lounge takes you to a bygone era. Grab a booth or a stool at the long marble-topped bar where flat-capped bar staff will mix you up Prohibition-era cocktails. It has a revolving liquor shelf that can be hidden with the press of a button, and a long menu of pre- and post-Prohibition cocktails. (☎021-5790 1295; Jl Tinju; cocktails from 120,000Rp; ⏰11am-1am Sun-Thu, to 2am Fri & Sat)

Lucy in the Sky

BAR

31 ⬤ MAP P116, B2

Head upstairs to this atrium rooftop garden space to soak up one of Jakarta's best party spots with fun-loving locals here for nightly DJs spinning anything from loud hip-hop to R&B. It's a great place to hang out, with retro furniture, pot plants and city views, and a good cocktail list including watermelon Moscow mules and mint martinis.

On Fridays and Saturdays there's a 500,000Rp cover charge, which is redeemable against drinks and food. (☎0813 1986 7542; www.lucyinthesky jakarta.com; Jl Jendral Sudirman Kav 52-53; beers/cocktails from 60,000/120,000Rp; ⏰4pm-1am Mon & Tue, to 3am Wed-Sun)

Amomali
COFFEE

32 MAP P116, E1

A well-respected coffee chain specialising in quality Indonesian beans prepared by expert baristas using Aeropress, V-60 pour-overs and espresso. It serves single origin brews including those from Papua New Guinea, Java, Bali and more. It's a cool little hang-out with polished concrete floors, good breakfasts and light mains (pasta, salads and *kung pao* chicken). (📞021-522 9228; http://store.anomali coffee.com; Setiabudi Bldg 1, Jl HR Rasuna Said, Lippo Kuningan; coffee 28,000Rp; 🕙6.30am-10.30pm Mon-Fri, 7am-10am Sat & Sun; 🛜)

Jakarta Coffee House
COFFEE

33 MAP P116, B8

One of the city's best spots for Indonesian single-origin coffee is this intimate micro-roastery with knowledgeable baristas who can prepare coffee to your tastes. They roast all their beans, sourced from Aceh to Papua, on-site. It's often full of young coffee aficionados acting cool and smoking up a storm. (📞021-7590 0570; www. jakartacoffeehouse.com; Jl Cipete Raya 2; coffee 27,000-100,000Rp; 🕙8am-midnight Sun-Thu, to 1am Fri & Sat; 🛜)

Trafique Coffee
COFFEE

34 MAP P116, A3

Set in a cavernous, industrial-chic space, this up-market coffee roaster specialises in Indonesian beans. Take your pick from pour-overs, filter or espresso, or try its 48-hour cold drip or nitro coffee on tap. It also does all-day breakfasts and burgers. (📞0878 8984 8004; Jl Hang Tuah Raya 9; 🕙9am-10pm; 🛜)

Liberica
COFFEE

Great hot beverages keep people seeking out the cafes in this mini-Jakarta chain (see 51 Map p116, B6). Natural wood details and the requisite top-end-coffee-house chalkboard create a warm and casual feel. At any time, there're baked goods and light meals (sandwiches, nachos and chicken quesadillas) on offer. (📞021-2952 9914; http://libericacoffee.com; Colony, Jl Kemang Raya 6A; menu items 56,000-98,000Rp; 🕙8am-11pm Sun-Thu, to 1am Fri & Sat)

Potato Head
BAR

An offshoot of the legendary Bali original, this brilliant warehouse-style bar-bistro with remarkable artistic decor (including a vertical garden and vintage seating) inside Pacific Place (see 48 Map p116, B2) also promotes music and cultural events. There are great cocktails, great grub (pork belly, fish, chilli garlic prawns) and a great outdoor terrace too. (📞021-5797 3322; www. pttthead.com/jakarta; Pacific Place, Jl Jenderal Sudirman 52-53; small plates from 65,000Rp, mains 95,000-255,000Rp; 🕙11.30am-midnight Sun-Thu, to 1.30am Fri & Sat; 🛜)

Eastern Promise
PUB

35 MAP P116, B5

A classic British-style pub in the heart of Kemang, serving Bintang,

Top Spots for Pampering: Spa Treats

South Jakarta offers a couple of top spas for bodily pampering. **Jamu Body Treatment** (Map p116, B8; 📞021-765 9691; www.jamu traditionalspa.com; Jl Cipete VIII/94B, Cipete; massage & treatments from 170,000Rp; ⏲9am-7pm) is an elegant place that uses *jamu* (Indonesian herbs with medicinal and restorative properties) for its treatments. Choose from scrubs, masks, wraps, reflexology, and warm stone and Balinese massages.

Soft music and perfumed air greet you at **Relax Living** (Map p116, E5; 📞021-719 4051; Jl Kemang Raya 2; 30min treatments 100,000Rp; ⏲10am-10pm Mon-Fri, 9am-10pm Sat & Sun), which offers a broad range of therapies and treatments. Feel the day's heat and weariness fade away. For pure decadence book a four-hand massage.

Heineken, Anker, Carlsberg and Guinness. It has a pool table, well-worn furnishings and filling international meals (from tenderloin steak to a dozen Indian dishes). There's live music and roast dinners on weekends. Sporting matches and quiz nights draw crowds. It's a legendary expat hang-out. (📞021-7179 0151; www.epjakarta.com; Jl Kemang Raya 5; mains 85,000-245,000Rp; ⏲10am-2am Sun-Thu, to 3am Fri & Sat; 📶)

Entertainment

Kinosaurus Jakarta CINEMA

36 ⭐ MAP P116, E6

Walk through the Aksara (p130) bookshop, then rub shoulders with Jakarta's artistic community at this hidden cinema, which hosts independent short and fringe films from around Indonesia and the world. Most are either in English or have English subtitles, but there are exceptions. Check the website for details of upcoming movies. (www.kinosaurusjakarta.com; Jl Kemang Raya 8B; tickets 50,000Rp; ⏲screenings usually 7pm & 9.30pm Fri, 4.30pm & 7pm Sat & Sun)

Nautilus LIVE MUSIC

37 ⭐ MAP P116, C3

Nautilus is a bold, classic Euro-Asian-bling drinking lounge at the Four Seasons hotel. Upon entering, you're drawn to the striking mural of the historic Sunda Kelapa (see p49) port behind the bar. There's live music (ranging from singers to jazz musicians, soul musicians and pianists) between 6pm and 9pm Tuesday to Saturday. (📞021-2277 1888; www.fourseasons.com/jakarta/dining/lounges/nautilus-bar; Four Seasons Hotel, Capital Pl, Jl Jendral Gatot Subroto Kav 18, Kuningan Barat; cocktails from 175,000Rp; ⏲noon-1am)

Gelora Bung Karno Stadium
STADIUM

38 ⭐ MAP P116, B1

Indonesia's largest stadium was completed in 1962. Since then it's had a few rebuildings and is presently used for football matches – especially by visiting European teams – and performances by popular groups before huge crowds. Its capacity was used for the 2018 Asian Games. (www.gelorabungkarno.co.id; Jl Pintu Satu Senayan)

Shopping

Pasar Santa
MARKET

39 🅐 MAP P116, B4

On the 2nd floor of a rundown old school mall you'll find Jakarta's hipster entrepreneurs. Dozens of individual booths sell everything from retro psychedelic clothing and vinyl to handmade jewellery, cakes, skateboards and artisanal coffee. The wackiest of the booths? A mini darkroom rental studio and a nitrogen ice-cream stall. Refuel with some tasty noodles at Mie Chino (p119). (Jl Cipaku I; ⏰hours vary Tue-Sun)

Aksara
BOOKS

40 🅐 MAP P116, E6

A wide selection of books (many in English) plus fine stationery and writing accessories make this hip hang-out a must-stop for anyone interested in words on paper. There's a small cafe serving coffee and cakes, plus a workshop offering various creative classes, including sessions in pottery and art, you can enquire within about schedules. (ak.'sa.ra; 📞021-719 9288; www.facebook.com/AksaraStore; Jl Kemang Raya 8; ⏰10am-10pm)

dia.lo.gue artspace
ART

41 🅐 MAP P116, C8

Contemporary art exhibitions, stylish designer goods, books, old travel posters and good coffee come together in this chic space. Bare concrete and glass are an ideal backdrop for the captivating variety here. Those who want to hang out longer stop at the trendy cafe on-site. (📞021-719 9671; https://dialogue-artspace.com; Jl Kemang Selatan 99; ⏰10am-10pm; 📶)

Past Future Sense
VINTAGE

Retro wear in all its glorious forms, from pre-owned Dr Martens and trainers to patterned shirts, caps, sew-on badges and jackets (see 27 🅐 Map p116, D7). Items are displayed on industrial metal railings, and there's a vintage arcade console in store for good measure. (📞021-718 3658; Jl Kemang Timur 998; ⏰noon-8pm)

Älska
GIFTS & SOUVENIRS

42 🅐 MAP P116, B8

This little shop was launched by esteemed Indonesian fashion photographer Nicoline Patricia Malina. Älska sells locally made and hand-picked international gifts, plus homewares. Browse the beautiful items ranging from terrariums to jewellery. (Jl Cipete Raya 7D; ⊙11am-9pm)

Biasa

CLOTHING

43 🅐 MAP P116, F7

Created by Italian-born designer Susanna Perini, the Biasa brand was inspired by Indonesian culture. Perini's style is up-market resort wear – loose warm-weather designs incorporating linen, light fabrics and vibrant colours. The modern, minimalist boutique spreads over two floors. (☎021-718 2322; http://biasagroup.com/collection; Jl Kemang Raya 20; ⊙9am-8pm)

Darmawangsa Square

MALL

44 🅐 MAP P116, A5

Like an up-market souk, this mall has a handful of local designers and smaller boutique-style shops. They're surrounded by marble floors, an intricate balcony, a palm-tree-lined shopping hall and a mesmerising blue skylight box overhead. (☎021-720 5066; Jl Darmawangsa VI; ⊙10am-10pm)

Lucy's Batik

GIFTS & SOUVENIRS

45 🅐 MAP P116, E7

Lucy's Batik has beautiful hand-made gifts, clothing and weavings, silver jewellery, wood crafts, home decor, furnishings and much more from across the archipelago. The company also runs ad hoc Indonesian craft workshops and gallery shows; ask in store for details. (☎021-2952 8536; www.lucysbatik.com; Lippo Mall Kemang, Jl Pangeran Antasari 36; ⊙10am-10pm)

Batik clothing

Ranch Market

FOOD & DRINKS

46 🔒 MAP P116, D2

Good-quality grocery selling fruit, veg, basic foods; lots of local and international brands. (📞021-2554 2493; Oakwood, Lingkar Mega Kuningan, Kuningan; ⏰8am-10pm)

Goods Dept

DEPARTMENT STORE

Lovers of streetwear will find a solid combination of local indie design wear and limited-edition Nike trainers at the Goods Dept, inside Pacific Place (see 48 🔒 Map p116, B2). Accessory racks are loaded with curated items, and there's plenty of gift potential: local jewellery brands, quirky stationery and other knick-knacks. (📞021-5797 3644; www.thegoodsdept. com; 1st fl, Pacific Place, Jl Jenderal Sudirman; ⏰10am-10pm; 📶)

Plaza Senayan

Tulisan

GIFTS & SOUVENIRS

47 🔒 MAP P116, A5

Tulisan is an Indonesian accessories label that specialises in brightly coloured illustrated prints and is best known for its playful canvas tote bags. The flagship store is a wonderful place for gifts, stocking a plentiful selection of quirky wall-hangings, illustrated paper goods, homewares and other oddities. Every product is handcrafted. (📞021-7278 0235; www.tulisan.com; ground fl, City Walk, Darmawangsa Sq, Jl Darmawangsa 9; ⏰9am-9pm)

ARA

CLOTHING

On the hunt for the best local fashion labels? Then head to ARA, a high-end concept store and independent fashion boutique inside Colony (see 51 🔒 Map p116, B6). There's no other shop quite like this in Jakarta, showcasing Indonesia's top up-and-coming talent alongside star designers like Sapto Djojokartiko and Peggy Hartanto. It also stocks locally made fine jewellery and trendy eye-wear. (📞021-2952 9958; www.arajakarta.com; Colony, Jl Kemang Raya 6; ⏰11am-8pm)

Pacific Place

MALL

48 🔒 MAP P116, B2

This huge midrange to high-end mall is anchored by the Parisian department store Galleries Lafayette. The complex includes luxury hotels and condos, up-market nightspots and more than 100 shops, including international fashion brands Montblanc, Hermès,

Hugo Boss, Prada and Victoria's Secret. It defines the cliché that is a South Jakarta megamall. (☏021-514 02828; www.pacificplace.co.id; JI Jenderal Sudirman; ⏱10am-10pm)

Blok M
MALL

49 🅰 MAP P116, A4

This mall is renowned for its cheap prices on a huge range of budget goods from phone covers and flip-flops (thongs) to T-shirts. Wander the endless corridors and expect to bargain. Head to the lower level for the huge food court. Outside you'll find a busy Transjakarta bus station. (☏021-726 0170; http://malblokm.com; JI Melawi; ⏱10am-10pm)

Kota Kasablanka
MALL

50 🅰 MAP P116, F2

This big midrange mall has high-street brands like Marks & Spencer, Top Shop, Zara and H&M. There's a range of beauty services on the lower level and dining options for most budgets spread out across the mall. There's also a cinema, plus a Carrefour supermarket. (www.kotakasablanka.co.id; JI Casablanca 88; ⏱10am-10pm)

Colony
MALL

51 🅰 MAP P116, B6

In a city splashed with flashy malls, this unusual, tall mall, with its understated, modest-sized collection of shops, stands out. There's a **Periplus** (www.periplus.com) bookshop, cafe Liberica (p128) –

attracting hipsters of all stripes – a rooftop restaurant, FJ on 7 (p123), a Toni & Guy and the very good ARA fashion boutique. (☏021-2952 9929; www.colony6kemang.com; JI Kemang Raya 6; ⏱10am-10pm)

Pasaraya
DEPARTMENT STORE

52 🅰 MAP P116, B4

Opposite the Blok M mall, this department store has two huge floors that seem to go on forever. The slogan here is 'The pride of Indonesia', and you'll see why when you discover the enormous range of handicrafts from areas throughout the archipelago. It's a fascinating place to browse; watch out for sales. Other outlets include branches of Converse and Djournal Coffee. (☏021-722 8470; www.pasaraya.co.id; JI Iskandarsyah II; ⏱10am-10pm)

Plaza Senayan
MALL

53 🅰 MAP P116, A2

A huge plaza with a cinema and shops including Gucci, Burberry, Victoria's Secret and Chanel, along with other big-bucks brands. Plus lots of cafes. (☏021-572 5555; www.plaza-senayan.com; JI Asia Afrika; ⏱10am-10pm; 🛜)

Qonita Batik
CLOTHING

54 🅰 MAP P116, F7

This locally well-regarded design store has its own line of clothing made with classic Javanese batik, including a large collection of colourful headscarves. (www.qonitabatik.com; JI Kemang Raya 27; ⏱9am-9pm)

Top Sight 📷
Jakarta's High-End Malls

Jakarta's many high-end malls are about more than just shopping. Across the south of the city are huge developments that combine large malls, cinemas, up-market hotels and condos. They feature major brands, as well as local labels and goods. Far from being the preserve of Jakarta's wealthy elite, in these malls you'll see Jakartans of all stripes endlessly browsing while enjoying the air-con and free entertainment.

🧍 If you're staying in central Jakarta, Plaza Indonesia and Grand Indonesia may be within walking distance.

🚗 From outside central Jakarta, it's best to access malls by taxi.

Plaza Indonesia

Near-constant renovations enable Menteng's original high-end mall (p94) to keep up with the pack. Here you'll find leading Indonesian boutiques as well as Toko Ampuh for local medicines and remedies and Batik Karis for high-quality Indonesian batik.

Grand Indonesia

This retail temple (p94) in Menteng covers eight marble-clad floors and two vast buildings linked by sky-bridges. It has a plethora of high-end fashion outlets, good local and international restaurants, and a multiscreen cinema.

Kota Kasablanka

Most budgets are accommodated at this big, generic South Jakarta mall (p133). The dozens of restaurants include an up-market food court on the lower level.

South Jakarta Malls

Pacific Place (pictured; p132) is anchored by the department store Galleries Lafayette and includes luxury hotels and condos, up-market nightspots and over 100 shops.

Uber-high-end Plaza Senayan (p133) offers familiar brand shops, including Marks & Spencer, Zara, Kate Spade and Bally. The icing on the cake is its luxury cinema. It has an even bigger counterpart opposite, Senayan City, which attracts the masses with chains like Gap.

★ Top Tips

○ At night and on weekends, many malls have free live entertainment in their cavernous main common areas. You may luck out with an Indonesian pop star, but more often you can expect crooning cover bands.

○ Jakarta also has over 170 non-luxury malls, such as Pasar Glodok (p54), selling more mundane items. These can be fascinating places to observe daily life.

○ Malls are haggle-free zones. But, depending on exchange rates, prices can be excellent.

✕ Take a Break

For fresh, tasty and cheap food, explore the furthest recesses of the malls. Usually there's a food court for workers where the spice levels and flavours are authentic, and the stalls family-run.

Top Sight Jakarta's High-End Malls

Worth a Trip 🔭
Bogor

As an oasis of unpredictable weather – it is credited with 322 thunderstorms a year – cool, quiet Bogor was the chosen retreat of colonials fleeing stifling, crowded Batavia. Today Bogor is an ideal day trip from Jakarta, even if the modern sprawl means you never quite escape the capital. The local people are warm and friendly, and the world-class botanical gardens beautiful.

Great Garden
www.krbogor.lipi.go.id
25,000Rp
🕑 7.30am-5pm

Pasar Baru

Jl Suryakencana, just steps from the garden gates, is a whirlwind of activity as shoppers spill en masse from within the byzantine concrete halls of **Pasar Baru** (cnr Jl Otto Iskandardinata & Jl Suryakencana; ⏲6am-1pm) onto the street. Inside, the morning market is awash with all manner of produce and flowers, meat and fish, secondhand clothes and more.

Kebun Raya

At the heart of Bogor are the fabulous botanical gardens (pictured), known as the Kebun Raya – the city's green lung of around 87 hectares. Governor-General Raffles originated the garden here; colonial cash crops, such as tea, cassava, tobacco and cinchona, were first grown here by Dutch botanists.

The gardens are said to contain 400 types of palms, including the footstool palm native to Indonesia, which tops 40m. There's a good stock of graceful pandan trees (look out for their unusual aerial roots). Drop by the Orchid House and take in the lovely, muddy ponds, which have dozens of giant water lilies over a metre across.

Crowds flock here on Sundays, but the gardens are quiet at most other times. The southern gate is the main entrance; other gates are only open on Sunday and holidays.

Istana Bogor

In the northwestern quadrant of the botanical gardens, the summer palace of the president was formerly the opulent official residence of the Dutch governors-general from 1870 to 1942. Today herds of white-spotted deer roam the immaculate lawns, and the building contains Sukarno's huge art collection, which largely focuses on the female figure. The palace is only open by prior arrangement, but the grounds are still worth a wander.

★ **Top Tips**

○ Allow yourself at least half a day to enjoy Kebun Raya.

✕ **Take a Break**

The **Grand Garden Café** (☎0251-857 4070; mains 45,000-105,000Rp; ⏲8am-11pm Sun-Thu, to midnight Fri & Sat) in Kebun Raya is a wonderfully civilised place for a bite or a drink, with sweeping views down to the water-lily ponds. It's a little pricey, but the tasty international and Indonesian food and sublime setting make it an essential stop.

★ **Getting There**

🚆 Express trains (6000-16,000Rp, 1 hour) connect Bogor with the capital roughly every hour, though try to avoid travelling during rush hour. Economy trains are more frequent, but they are packed with people.

Survival Guide

Street food vendor PHOTOSGENIQUES/SHUTTERSTOCK ©

Before You Go

Book Your Stay

○ Jakarta has many good hotels and they are seldom full. Even better, prices are low compared to other large Asian cities, so you may be able to give yourself an upgrade.

○ Budget travellers will find some fine hostels, while long-term visitors will have many apartment-style hotels to choose from.

○ Swimming pools tend to be limited to more expensive places.

○ Higher end hotels may tax at 21% (a combined tax and service charge called 'plus plus').

Useful Websites

Lonely Planet (lonelyplanet.com/ indonesia/jakarta/ hotels) Recommendations and bookings.

Bayu Buana Travel (www.bayubuana travel.com) Provides a wide range of hotels on its booking portal website.

Jakarta

When to Go

○ **Rainy Season (Oct-May)**

There is no time of year when you can be assured of dry weather in tropical Jakarta but during these months you can expect it to rain more than half the time. Deluges can be intense, so plan accordingly.

○ **Dry Season (Jun-Sep)**

People visit Jakarta year-round for business. There is an uptick in tourists in August during the European and North American summer, but the numbers are not enough to make a difference in terms of finding accommodation etc.

Panorama JTB (www. panorama-jtb.com) Budget and midrange hotel options.

Best Budget

Six Degrees (www. jakarta-backpackers-hostel.com) A very comfortable hostel with a garden.

Packer Lodge (www. thepackerlodge.com) Hip hostel in a great location in Glodok.

Capsule Hotel Old Batavia (http://capsule hoteloldbatavia.jakarta hotels.site) Friendly and clean, with super-helpful staff.

Best Midrange

Hotel Akmani (http:// akmanihotel.com) A high-rise hotel with a mod design.

Hotel Dreamtel (www. dreamteljakarta.com) Well-equipped rooms in a striking high-rise.

Ibis Budget Hotel Cikini (www.ibis.com) Top location near hip coffee shops and sights.

Best Top End

Artotel Thamrin (www.artotelindonesia.com) Floors are decorated by eight Indonesian artists; there's nowhere else quite like this.

Morrissey (http://iammorrissey.co) Large apartment-style rooms in a designer package with a great location.

Hotel Indonesia Kempinski (www.kempinski.com) Surrounded by malls, with sweeping city views.

Best for Families

DoubleTree by Hilton (www.doubletree.hilton.com) Moderately priced hotel with a Kids' Club.

Hotel Indonesia Kempinski (www.kempinski.com) Has a special playground for children.

Hotel Borobudur Jakarta (https://hotelborobudur.com) An older luxe hotel with huge grounds, an enormous pool and a playground.

Best Stylish Hotels

Artotel Thamrin (www.artotelindonesia.com) A visually arresting

hotel with each floor designed by a top Indonesian artist.

Kosenda Hotel (www.kosendahotel.com) A hip hotel with a good terrace and a rooftop bar.

Kemang Icon Hotel (www.kemangiconhotels.com) Cutting-edge design and amenities in an intimate hotel with only 12 rooms.

Arriving in Jakarta

Soekarno-Hatta International Airport

⊙ All international flights and most domestic flights operate from **Soekarno-Hatta International Airport** (CGK; http://soekarnohatta-airport.co.id; Tangerang City), 35km west of the city centre. Surging passenger numbers mean that it can get chaotic, so give yourself plenty of time for formalities.

⊙ There are three terminals, each with a full range of facilities, such as ATMs, information desks and exchange

counters. It's vital to confirm which terminal your flight will depart from as terminals are not close to each other. A free shuttle service operates between the three terminals.

Terminal 1 The hub for many domestic flights.

Terminal 2 Used for both international and domestic flights.

Terminal 3 The hub for international flights.

⊙ A toll road links the airport to the city and the journey takes one to two hours depending on traffic and the final destination.

⊙ **Damri** (www.busbandara.com; Gambir Station; airport 40,000Rp) airport buses run every 15 minutes between 4am and 10pm between the airport and **Gambir train station** (Jl Medan Merdeka Timur 1), along with several other points in the city including Blok M (p116), Tanjung Priok and **Kampung Rambutan bus terminal**.

⊙ A new **Railink** (https://reservation.railink.co.id) connects the airport with city stations Manggarai, Sudirman Baru, Duri and Batu Ceper.

o Taxis from the airport to Jl Thamrin/Jl Jaksa cost around 220,000Rp including tolls. Be sure to book via the official taxi desks, rather than using the unlicensed drivers outside. Grab can drop off passengers, but are prohibited from airport pick-ups. You may be able to meet a Grab driver if you walk up beyond airport perimeters.

Halim Perdana Kusama Airport

o **Halim Perdana Kusama Airport** (HLP; www.halimperdanakusama-airport.co.id) is 11km south of Jakarta's Cikini district. It has limited domestic services.

o The airport is not served well by pubic transport. A taxi is the easiest and most reliable option from central Jakarta, costing around 120,000Rp, depending on your pick-up area and traffic.

o Note, if you're travelling from Soekarno-Hatta International Airport (CGK) and hope to catch a flight out of HLP, the transfer can take one to three hours depending on traffic

in central Jakarta. The journey costs around 230,000Rp in a taxi.

o An express train connecting the two airports is expected to be completed by late 2019.

Tanjung Priok

o Pelni shipping services operate on sporadic schedules to ports all over the archipelago. The **Pelni ticketing office** (📞021-162; www.pelni.co.id; Jl Gajah Mada 14; ⏰8am-4.30pm Mon-Fri) is 1.5km northwest of the Monumen Nasional in central Jakarta.

o Pelni ships all arrive at and depart from Pelabuhan Satu (dock 1) at Tanjung Priok, 13km northeast of the city centre. Transjakarta *koridor* (busway lines) 10 and 12 provide a direct bus link. Single fares start at 2000Rp; routes and bus arrivals vary wildly depending on traffic. A taxi from Jl Jaksa costs between 70,000Rp and 120,000Rp.

Bus Stations

Jakarta has four major bus terminals, all a long way from the city

centre. The Transjakarta busway to these terminals uses bus lanes; a car journey can take hours in traffic. Tickets (some including travel to the terminals) for the better buses can be bought from agencies (like www.redbus.id/en or www.easybook.com).

o **Kalideres** (Jl Daan Mogot) Serves points west of Jakarta, but services were greatly reduced at the time of research. Take Transjakarta bus line 3 or 2A to get here.

o **Kampung Rambutan** (Rambutan) Mainly handles buses to points south and southwest of Jakarta such as Bogor. It's also possible to get buses to Cepu, Jepara, Surabaya and Denpasar from here.

o **Terminal Pulogadung** (Jl Raya Bekasi; 📶) Covers Bandung, central and east Java, Sumatra, Bali and even Nusa Tenggara.

o **Lebak Bulus** (Jl Lebak Bulus Raya) Runs bus routes to Blok M, Senen and Kota, plus other citywide locations. Lebak Bulus Station is also on the Jakarta MRT route, which should be fully operational during 2019.

Train

Jakarta's four main train stations are quite central. Services (www.kereta-api.co.id) run to cities around Jakarta and across Java, and train travel is the most convenient way to leave the city. You can also book via booking agencies Tiket (https://en.tiket.com) and Traveloka (www.traveloka.com/en) and can even get a train–ferry–bus connection to Bali. Fares are cheap, so it can be worth buying the best available class of service.

○ **Gambir** (Jl Medan Merdeka Timur 1) is the most convenient and important of Jarkarta's train stations. It's on the eastern side of Merdeka Square, a 15-minute walk from Jl Jaksa. It handles express trains to Bandung, Yogyakarta, Solo, Semarang and Surabaya. It is a well-run and modern facility with full services and a good place to buy tickets.

○ **Jakarta Kota** (Jl Asemka) is an art-deco gem in its namesake

neighbourhood. It has limited services and commuter trains to greater Jakarta areas and Bogor.

○ **Pasar Senen** (Jl Bungur Besar) to the east mostly has economy-class trains to the east and south.

○ **Tanah Abang** (THB; Jl Jati Baru Raya) offers economy trains to the west.

Getting Around

Bicycle

○ Best for exploring local neighbourhoods

○ Jakarta's devilish traffic and lack of real bike lanes makes getting around by bicycle very difficult outside mostly traffic-free tourist areas within Kota.

○ However, many cyclists take to the streets on **Car Free Day** (www.infocarfreeday.net; Jl Sudirman & Jl Thamrin; free; ⊙6-11am Sun), which occurs every Sunday morning (6am to 11am) between the main streets of Jl Sudirman and Jl MH Thamrin.

Bus

○ Best for getting around the city relatively quickly.

○ Transjakarta is a network of air-conditioned buses that run on reserved busways (designated lanes that are closed to all other traffic). They are the quickest way to get around the city.

○ One of the most useful routes is koridor (busway line) 1, which runs north to Kota, past Monas and along Jl Sudirman. Stations display maps (www.transjakarta.co.id/peta-rute).

○ Most busways have been constructed in the centre of existing highways, and stations have been positioned at roughly 1km intervals. Access is via elevated walkways and each station has a shelter. Fifteen koridor are up and running.

○ Fares cost 3500Rp to 9000Rp, which covers any destination in the network (regardless of how many koridor you use). Payment is via a stored-value card (40,000Rp, including 20,000Rp credit), which is available from

Tuk-tuks

Tuk-tuks are everywhere in central Jakarta. They're often a little faster than other modes of transport, due to being able to negotiate small gaps in the traffic. However, fares need to be negotiated, and tourists can end up paying more than the price of a metered taxi.

station ticket windows. Note that you can share the card with others, so there's no need to purchase more than one if travelling in a group.

o Most buses run from 5am to 10pm and are often very crowded. Also during rush hour, some vehicles are diverted onto the busways, which clogs progress.

o There are seven 24-hour bus services – *koridor* 1, 9, 3, 2, 5, 8 and 10. Their frequency is (in theory) between 30 minutes and 60 minutes, traffic permitting.

o Schedules vary greatly, it's best to leave extra time for every journey. Buses very rarely run to schedule, due to traffic.

Car & Motorcycle

o Best for navigating Jakarta's chaotic and poorly marked streets.

o Major international car-rental firms have offices at the airport and in the city.

o Most people opt for a car with a driver, who can navigate Jakarta's roads. These can be arranged through your hotel (from 500,000Rp to 700,000Rp per day) or via the **Grab** (www. grab.com) app. Fuel, but not tolls or parking, is included in the price.

o In an effort to curb the sclerotic traffic, cars with odd and even licence plate numbers are banned from entering the city on alternate days.

o With suitable bravery, you can hop on a motorcycle *(ojek)* and join Jakarta's traffic, but it is not for the inexperienced. A better option is to grab a **Go-Jek** (☎021-725 1110; www.go-jek.com) or **Grab** (www.grab.com) bike. Both companies

operate an app-based service and provide helmets. A short ride will be about 25,000Rp.

Taxi & Motorbike Taxi

Getting about Jakarta on a motorbike taxi is quicker than other options. However, you will be exposed to the city's air pollution and it's obviously less safe.

o Taxis are inexpensive in Jakarta. All are metered and flag fall is 7500Rp, then it's around 300Rp for each subsequent 100m after the first kilometre.

o Tipping is greatly appreciated.

o Most taxi drivers don't speak English. It helps to have your destination written in Bahasa or to show them on a map.

o Not all taxis provide good service. The most reliable taxis are run by **Blue Bird** (☎021-794 1234; www.bluebirdgroup. com); they can be found cruising, at cab stands and at many hotels. Order one using its handy app.

o Singapore-based **Grab** (www.grab.com), which

acquired Uber, offers ride services that can be remarkably cheap (around US$30 for eight hours driving around town). Order and manage your rides through its apps. Note that there's no guarantee your driver will speak any English. Tolls and parking fees are extra.

Subway & Monorail

The new **Jakarta MRT** (☎ 021-390 6454; www.jakartamrt.co.id), plus a monorail, **Jakarta LRT** (www.adhi.co.id/en), are expected to be operational during 2019. They will run along a spine from Kota in the north via Jl Thamrin to Blok M in the south.

Essential Information

Accessible Travel

o Indonesia is a difficult destination for those with access issues, such as limited mobility, vision or hearing.

o Very few buildings in Jakarta have disabled access, and even international chain hotels may not have fully accessible facilities.

o Pavements are riddled with potholes, loose man-holes, parked motorcycles and all sorts of street life, and are very rarely level for long until the next set of steps. Even the able bodied walk on roads rather than negotiate the hassle of the pavement.

o However, as in many developing countries, Indonesians are extremely helpful and welcoming, so no wheelchair-using traveller will wait for long in front of a step without someone coming to help.

o Public transport is entirely inaccessible for wheelchair users. Cars with a driver can be hired readily at cheap rates, but wheelchair-accessible vehicles can only be arranged through specialist accessible tour operators.

o Taman Fatahillah in Old Jakarta and the old port of Sunda Kelapa are relatively accessible for wheelchair users.

o Most four- and five-star hotels have one or two accessible rooms with basic accessible facilities, but it's best to call ahead to make sure that the room will meet your needs.

o Motionaid (8788 219 2701; www.motionaid.co.id) has a vehicle with a wheelchair lift and swivel seat for hire.

o The owners of Accessible Indonesia (www.accessibleindonesia.org) are knowledgeable and well connected, and work with local disability organisations. They offer tours principally to Java, Sulawesi and Bali, as well as day cruises, diving and snorkelling expeditions, and wheelchair-accessible transfers. They are well used to problem-solving to overcome infrastructural barriers. There is access information for international airports and basic access information about the destinations they serve on their website.

o Download Lonely Planet's free Accessible Travel guides from http://lptravel.to/AccessibleTravel.

Business Hours

Banks 8am–2pm Mondays to Thursdays, 8am–noon Fridays, 8am–11am Saturdays

Government offices
8am–3pm Mondays to Thursdays, 8am–noon Fridays

Museums Usually closed Mondays

Post offices 8am–2pm Mondays to Fridays

Private businesses
8am–4pm or 9am–5pm Mondays to Fridays, to noon Saturdays

Restaurants usually 8am–10pm

Shopping 10am–8pm; larger shops and malls to 10pm. Some closed Sundays.

Electricity

Type C
220V/50Hz

Type F
230V/50Hz

Money

ATMs

ATMs are common in Jakarta.

Currency

The unit of currency is the rupiah (Rp). Coins of 50Rp, 100Rp, 200Rp, 500Rp and 1000Rp are in circulation. Notes come in 2000Rp, 5000Rp, 10,000Rp, 20,000Rp, 50,000Rp and 100,000Rp denominations.

Credit Cards

Accepted at midrange and better hotels and resorts. More expensive restaurants and shops will also accept them, but look out for a sur-charge of around 3%.

Changing Money

o The US dollar is the most widely accepted foreign currency. The Australian dollar, pound sterling, euro and the Japanese yen are also exchangeable.

o Use airports, banks, reputable currency exchanges and hotels.

o Never use street-side counters or individuals: scams abound.

Guide Exchange Rates

Australia	A$1	10,000Rp
Canada	C$1	10,630Rp
Europe	€1	16,100Rp
Japan	¥100	12,700Rp
NZ	NZ$1	9700Rp
UK	UK£1	18,700Rp
USA	US$1	14,200Rp

For current exchange rates, see www.xe.com.

Tipping

o Tipping a set amount is not expected, but a tip of 5000Rp to 10,000Rp (or 10% of the total bill) is highly appreciated.

o Hand cash directly to individuals (taxi drivers, porters, people giving you a massage etc) to

Money-Saving Tips

Visitors can get tax refunds on purchases over 500,000Rp. Look out for the VAT Refund logos in store or ask at high-end shops for details.

recognise their service.

o Most midrange and all top-end hotels and restaurants add 21% to the bill for tax and service (called 'plus plus').

Public Holidays

Listed below are the national public holidays in Indonesia. Unless stated, they vary from year to year.

Tahun Baru Masehi (New Year's Day) 1 January

Tahun Baru Imlek (Chinese New Year) Late January to early February

Wafat Yesus Kristus (Good Friday) Late March to mid-April

Hari Buruh (Labour Day) 1 May

Hari Waisak (Buddha's birth, enlightenment and death) May

Kenaikan Yesus Kristus (Ascension of Christ) May

Hari Proklamasi Kemerdekaan (Independence Day) 17 August

Hari Natal (Christmas Day) 25 December

The following Islamic holidays have dates that change each year.

Isra Miraj Nabi Muhammad Ascension of the Prophet Muhammad; around April.

Idul Fitri Also known as Lebaran, this two-day national public holiday marks the end of Ramadan; avoid travel due to crowds. Occurs around June.

Idul Adha Islamic feast of the sacrifice; around September.

Muharram Islamic New Year; around September.

Maulud Nabi Muhammad Birthday of the Prophet Muhammad; around December.

Safe Travel

Although some foreign embassies warn against travel to Indonesia, and especially Jakarta, overall there's little risk for travellers. For such a huge city with obvious social problems, it is surprisingly safe.

o Exercise more caution after dark/late at night in Glodok and Kota, where there are some seedy clubs and bars.

o Robberies by taxi drivers have been known to take place, so always opt for reputable firms and app-booking services such as the citywide Bluebird group, Grab or Go-Jek.

o Jakarta's buses and trains can be crowded, particularly during rush hours, which is when pickpockets are about.

Telephone

o Country Code ☏62

o The international access code can be any of three versions – try all three:

☏001; ☏008; ☏017

Emergency

Police ☏110
Fire ☏113
Medical Emergencies ☏119

Mobile Phones

o All new SIM cards bought in Indonesia must be registered. If you buy your card from an official shop of a mobile phone provider or at the airports in Jakarta, they will do it for you automatically.

o SIM cards start at 15,000Rp. They come with cheap rates for calling other countries, from around 5000Rp per minute.

o SIM cards are widely available and easily refilled with credit.

o Most official outlets offer deals where you pay 50,000Rp and up for a SIM card and credit.

o 4G networks are spreading across the nation, but speeds are slower than other countries.

o Data plans average about 40,000Rp for 1GB of data.

o Mobile numbers start with a four-digit prefix that begins with 08 and has a total of 10 to 12 digits.

Toilets

The few public toilets are usually squat and conditions are often unclean. Clean Western-style toilets are found in hotels, restaurants, malls and some museums.

LGBT+ Travellers

Gay and lesbian travellers in Indonesia should follow the same precautions as straight travellers: avoid public displays of affection. However, as the nation is becoming more conservative, any form of closeness between people of the same sex may be unwise.

o Gay men in Indonesia are referred to as *homo* or *gay;* lesbians are *lesbi.*

o Indonesia's community of transgender/transsexual *waria* – from the words *wanita* (woman) and *pria* (man) – has always had a very public profile; it's also known by the less polite term *banci.*

o Islamic groups proscribe homosexuality, but queer-bashing is uncommon.

o GAYa Nusantara (www.gayanusantara.or.id) has a very useful website that covers local LGBTQI issues.

Tourist Information

Jakarta Visitor Information Office (Map p100, B3; 021-316 1293, 021-314 2067; www.jakarta-tourism.go.id; Jl KH Wahid Hasyim 9; 7am-6pm) Private, very helpful tourism agency. Staff can book tours, flights and hotels (helpful as transport providers often require a local bankcard).

Visas

The visa situation is constantly in flux. It is essential that you confirm current formalities before you arrive.

Fines for overstaying your visa expiration date are 300,000Rp per day for the first 60 days, although there are rumours that may be increased. Overstay more and you will be deported and blacklisted from entering Indonesia, but you don't have to pay a fine.

Listed below are the main visa options that applied at the time of research.

Dos & Don'ts

Indonesia is a pretty relaxed place, but there are a few rules of etiquette.

Places of worship Be respectful in sacred places. Remove shoes and dress modestly when visiting mosques.

Body language Use both hands when handing somebody something. Don't show displays of affection in public or talk with your hands on your hips (it's seen as a sign of aggression).

Clothing Avoid showing a lot of skin, although many local men wear shorts. Don't go topless at any pool or beach if you're a woman.

Photography Before taking photos of someone, ask – or mime – for permission.

Alcohol Because drinking is becoming more controversial, only consume alcoholic beverages in designated places like bars and lounges.

Visa in Advance

Visitors can apply for a visa before they arrive in Indonesia. Typically this is a visitor's visa, which is usually valid for 60 days. Details vary by country; contact your nearest Indonesian embassy or consulate to determine processing fees and times. It is nearly always easiest to apply for this visa in your home country. Some Indonesian embassies are reluctant to grant these visas to non-nationals or non-residents of the country you are applying in. In Southeast Asia, Bangkok and Singapore are the most hassle-free places to apply for a 60-day visa. Note: this is the only way to obtain a 60-day visitor visa, even if you qualify for Visa on Arrival.

Visa on Arrival

This 30-day extendable visa is available at major airports and harbours (but not most land borders). The cost is US$35; be sure to have the exact amount in US currency. Eligible countries include Australia, Canada, much of the EU (including France, Germany, Ireland, the Netherlands and the UK), New Zealand and the USA. VOA renewals for 30 days are possible. If you don't qualify for VOA, you must get a visa in advance.

Visa Free

Citizens of 169 countries can receive a 30-day visa for free upon arrival. But note that this visa cannot be extended and you may be limited to which airports and ports you can use to exit the country.

Language

Indonesian, or Bahasa Indonesia as it is known to the locals, is the official language of Indonesia.

Indonesian pronunciation is easy to master. Each letter always represents the same sound and most letters are pronounced the same as their English counterparts. Just remember that *c* is pronounced as the 'ch' in 'chat' and *sy* as the 'sh' in 'ship'. Note also that *kh* is a throaty sound (like the 'ch' in the Scottish *loch*), and that the *ng* and *ny* combinations, which are also found in English at the end or in the middle of words such as 'ringing' and 'canyon' respectively, can also appear at the beginning of words in Indonesian.

Syllables generally carry equal emphasis – the main exception is the unstressed *e* in words such as *besar* (big) – but the rule of thumb is to stress the second-last syllable.

To enhance your trip with a phrasebook, visit lonelyplanet. com. Lonely Planet iPhone phrasebooks are available through the Apple App store.

Basics

Hello	*Salam.*
Goodbye. (if leaving)	*Selamat tinggal.*
Goodbye. (if staying)	*Selamat jalan.*
How are you?	*Apa kabar?*
I'm fine, and you?	*Kabar baik, Anda bagaimana?*
Excuse me.	*Permisi.*
Sorry.	*Maaf.*
Please.	*Silahkan.*
Thank you.	*Terima kasih.*
You're welcome.	*Kembali.*
Yes.	*Ya.*
No.	*Tidak.*
Mr/Sir	*Bapak*
Ms/Mrs/Madam	*Ibu*
Miss	*Nona*
What's your name?	*Siapa nama Anda?*
My name is ...	*Nama saya ...*
Do you speak English?	*Bisa berbicara Bahasa Inggris?*
I don't understand.	*Saya tidak mengerti.*

Eating & Drinking

What would you recommend?	*Apa yang Anda rekomendasikan?*
What's in that dish?	*Hidangan itu isinya apa?*
That was delicious.	*Ini enak sekali.*
Cheers!	*Bersulang!*
Bring the bill/ check, please.	*Tolong bawa kuitansi.*

I don't eat ...	*Saya tidak makan*
dairy products	*susu dan keju*
fish	*ikan*
(red) meat	*daging (merah)*
peanuts	*kacang tanah*
seafood	*makanan laut*
a table ...	*meja ...*
at (eight) o'clock	*pada jam (delapan)*
for (two) people	*untuk (dua) orang*

Key Words

baby food (formula)	*susu kaleng*
bar	*bar*
bottle	*botol*
bowl	*mangkuk*
breakfast	*sarapan*
cafe	*kafe*
children's menu	*menu untuk anak-anak*
cold	*dingin*
dinner	*makan malam*
dish	*piring*
drink list	*daftar minuman*
food	*makanan*
food stall	*warung*
fork	*garpu*
glass	*gelas*
highchair	*kursi tinggi*
hot (warm)	*hangat*
knife	*pisau*
lunch	*makan siang*
menu	*daftar makanan*
market	*pasar*
napkin	*tisu*

plate	*piring*
restaurant	*rumah makan*
salad	*selada*
soup	*sop*
spicy	*pedas*
spoon	*sendok*
vegetarian food	*makanan tanpa daging*
with	*dengan*
without	*tanpa*

Meat & Fish

beef	*daging sapi*
carp	*ikan mas*
chicken	*ayam*
duck	*bebek*
fish	*ikan*
lamb	*daging anak domba*
meat	*daging*
pork	*daging babi*
shrimp/prawn	*udang*
tuna	*cakalang*

Fruit & Vegetables

apple	*apel*
banana	*pisang*
beans	*kacang*
cabbage	*kol*
carrot	*wortel*
cauliflower	*blumkol*
cucumber	*timun*
eggplant	*terung*
fruit	*buah*

lemon	*jeruk asam*
orange	*jeruk manis*
potato	*kentang*
spinach	*bayam*
vegetable	*sayur-mayur*

Shopping

I'd like to buy ...	*Saya mau beli ...*
I'm just looking.	*Saya lihat-lihat saja.*
May I look at it?	*Boleh saya lihat?*
I don't like it.	*Saya tidak suka.*
How much is it?	*Berapa harganya?*
It's too expensive.	*Itu terlalu mahal.*
Can you lower the price?	*Boleh kurang?*

Emergencies

Help!	*Tolong saya!*
I'm lost.	*Saya tersesat.*
Leave me alone!	*Jangan ganggu saya!*
Call a doctor!	*Panggil dokter!*
Call the police!	*Panggil polisi!*
I'm ill.	*Saya sakit.*
It hurts here.	*Sakitnya di sini.*
I'm allergic to (antibiotics).	*Saya alergi (antibiotik).*

Time & Numbers

What time is it?	*Jam berapa sekarang?*
It's (10) o'clock.	*Jam (sepuluh).*
It's half to (seven; 6.30)	*Setengah (tujuh).*
in the morning	*pagi*

in the afternoon	*siang*
in the evening	*malam*
yesterday	*kemarin*
today	*hari ini*
tomorrow	*besok*

Monday	*hari Senin*
Tuesday	*hari Selasa*
Wednesday	*hari Rabu*
Thursday	*hari Kamis*
Friday	*hari Jumat*
Saturday	*hari Sabtu*
Sunday	*hari Minggu*

1	*satu*
2	*dua*
3	*tiga*
4	*empat*
5	*lima*
6	*enam*
7	*tujuh*
8	*delapan*
9	*sembilan*
10	*sepuluh*
20	*dua puluh*
30	*tiga puluh*
40	*empat puluh*
50	*lima puluh*
60	*enam puluh*
70	*tujuh puluh*
80	*delapan puluh*
90	*sembilan puluh*
100	*seratus*
1000	*seribu*

Transport & Directions

bicycle-rickshaw	becak
boat (local)	perahu
bus	bis
minibus	bemo
motorcycle-rickshaw	bajaj
motorcycle-taxi	ojek
plane	pesawat
taxi	taksi
train	kereta api
I want to go to	Saya mau ke
At what time does it leave?	Jam berapa berangkat?
At what time does it arrive at...?	Jam berapa sampai di...?
Does it stop at ...?	Di ... berhenti?
Please tell me when we get to...	Tolong, beritahu waktu kita sampai di...
Please stop here.	Tolong, berhenti di sini.
a ... ticket	tiket ...
1st-class	kelas satu
2nd-class	kelas dua
one-way	sekali jalan
return	pulang pergi
first/last	pertama/terakhir
platform	peron
ticket office	loket tiket
timetable	jadwal
train station	stasiun kereta api

Where is ...?	Di mana ...?
What's the address?	Alamatnya di mana?
Could you write it down, please?	Anda bisa tolong tuliskan?
Can you show me (on the map)?	Anda bisa tolong tunjukkan pada saya (di peta)?
at the corner	di sudut
at the traffic lights	di lampu merah
behind	di belakang
in front of	di depan
far (from)	jauh (dari)
left	kiri
near (to)	dekat (dengan)
next to	di samping
opposite	di seberang
right	kanan
straight ahead	lurus

Signs

Buka	Open
Dilarang	Prohibited
Kamar Kecil	Toilets
Keluar	Exit
Masuk	Entrance
Pria	Men
Tutup	Closed
Wanita	Women

Behind the Scenes

Send Us Your Feedback

We love to hear from travellers – your comments help make our books better. We read every word, and we guarantee that your feedback goes straight to the authors. Visit **lonelyplanet.com/contact** to submit your updates and suggestions.

Note: We may edit, reproduce and incorporate your comments in Lonely Planet products such as guidebooks, websites and digital products, so let us know if you don't want your comments reproduced or your name acknowledged. For a copy of our privacy policy visit lonelyplanet.com/privacy.

Jade's Thanks

Thanks to Destination Editor Tanya Parker for her support, knowledge and quick-fire responses on Jakarta. Plus, the wider Indonesia team and everyone working behind the scenes on this project – Cheree Broughton, Neill Coen, Evan Godt and Helen Elfer. Last but not least, thanks to the friendly Jakarta locals, who always remain calm, polite and helpful despite the endlessly chaotic surroundings of the city.

Acknowledgements

Cover photograph: Traditional market in slow-speed Jakarta, Herianus/Getty Images ©.

Photographs on pp 34-35 (clockwise from left): leodaphne/Shutterstock ©, Takashi Images/Shutterstock ©, Creativa Images/Shutterstock ©

This Book

This 2nd edition of Lonely Planet's *Pocket Jakarta* guidebook was curated by Simon Richmond, and researched and written by Jade Bremner. Stuart Butler researched and wrote about Bogor. The previous edition was written by Ryan Ver Berkmoes and curated by Simon Richmond. This guidebook was produced by the following:

Destination Editor
Tanya Parker

Senior Product Editor
Kate Chapman

Regional Senior Cartographer
Julie Sheridan

Product Editor
Claire Rourke

Book Designer
Clara Monitto

Assisting Editors
Andrew Bain, James Bainbridge, Michelle Bennett, Nigel Chin, Lucy Cowie, Melanie Dankel, Samantha Forge, Carly Hall, Lou McGregor, Rosie Nicholson, Sarah Reid, Jessica Ryan, Gabrielle Stefanos, Simon Williamson

Assisting Cartographer
Katerina Pavkova

Cover Researcher
Naomi Parker

Thanks to Jennifer Carey, Sasha Drew, Evan Godt, Martin Heng, Lauren Keith, Claire Naylor, Karyn Noble, Tayana Nuraida, Genna Patterson, Matt Phillips, Mazzy Prinsep, Eleanor Simpson, James Smart, Colin Whitefield

Index

See also separate subindexes for:

⊗ **Eating p157**

◯ **Drinking p158**

✪ **Entertainment p159**

🔒 **Shopping p159**

Our Writers

Simon Richmond

Journalist and photographer Simon Richmond has specialised as a travel writer since the early 1990s and first worked for Lonely Planet in 1999 on the Central Asia guide. He's long since stopped counting the number of guidebooks he's researched and written for the company, but countries covered include Australia, China, India, Iran, Japan, Korea, Malaysia, Mongolia, Myanmar (Burma), Russia, Singapore, South Africa and Turkey.

Jade Bremner

Jade has been a journalist for more than a decade. She has lived in and reported on four different regions. Wherever she goes she finds action sports to try, the weirder the better, and it's no coincidence many of her favourite places have some of the best waves in the world. Jade has edited travel magazines and sections for *Time Out* and *The Radio Times* and has contributed to *The Times,* CNN and *The Independent*. She feels privileged to share tales from this wonderful planet we call home and is always looking for the next adventure.

Contributing Writer

Stuart Butler contributed to the Bogar Worth a Trip.

Published by Lonely Planet Global Limited
CRN 554153
2nd edition – July 2019
ISBN 978 1 78657 846 4
© Lonely Planet 2019 Photographs © as indicated 2019
10 9 8 7 6 5 4 3 2 1
Printed in Singapore